The Little Auto

Guillaume Apollinaire (1880–1918) – whose writings ranged from plays to experimental poetry, from art criticism to erotica – was a central figure in the literary and artistic life of early 20th-century Paris. Both his work and his flamboyant personality had a defining influence on the development of Surrealism, Dadaism and other artistic movements.

Beverley Bie Brahic is a poet and translator. A Canadian, she lives in Paris and Stanford, California. Her translation of selected poems by Francis Ponge, *Unfinished Ode to Mud* (CBe, 2008) was shortlisted for the 2009 Popescu Prize for European poetry in translation; her poetry collection *White Sheets*, published by CBe in 2012, was shortlisted for the Forward Prize.

GUILLAUME
APOLLINAIRE

The Little Auto

translated by
Beverley Bie Brahic

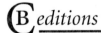 *editions*

Thanks to the editors of *Ambit*,
where some of these translations first appeared.

First published in 2012
by CB editions
146 Percy Road London W12 9QL
www.cbeditions.com

Printed in England by Blissetts, London W3 8DH

ISBN 978–0–9567359–4–2

Contents

Introduction

Apollinaire was never meant to live an ordinary life. Born Guillaume-Albert-Wladimir-Alexandre-Apollinaire-Kostrowitzky in Rome on 26 August 1880 of an unknown father (the candidates include a Catholic prelate and a Bourbon officer) and a Polish mother whose own adventurous life has the makings of romantic fiction, opening, say, with her ejection from a convent at the age of sixteen. Six years later Guillaume was born, and two years after that, his brother Albert, births registered as 'of parents unknown'. From 1885, Madame de Kostrowitzky travelled in Europe; but Guillaume was soon enrolled in school in Monaco, then Cannes and Nice, where he won prizes for his scholastic and artistic excellence, and signed his first poems 'Guillaume Apollinaire'. In 1899, moving with his mother and brother to Paris, he found work in a bank, and as French tutor to a German family whose travels took him to Germany, Vienna and Prague, and led him to meet and fall in love with the family's English governess, 'Annie'. Generous in friendship, prompt to love, Apollinaire seems to have charmed most people he met, though he was rejected in the end by 'Annie', who fled to Texas (his rueful poem begins 'On the coast of Texas/ Between Mobile and Galveston . . .'), and later by the painter Marie Laurencin, who left him for a German painter. He was a bon-vivant with his heart on his sleeve, a man of letters whose letters turned into poems, author of outrageous erotic tales, member of the Paris avant-garde (friends with the Cubist painters Picasso and Braque, and with Matisse, whose aesthetics he helped through his criticism to define); and, from 1914 to 1918, when he died, he was a soldier.

A 'war poet', Apollinaire? After all, he is so much better known as a proto-Surrealist experimenter with language, or Simultaneist, as he liked to say, thinking how his Cubist friends depicted scenes and figures all at once, collapsing space and time. Still, five of the six sections in Apollinaire's still startling third, 1918, volume of poems, *Calligrammes*, were composed while he was on the front lines in World War I. It is tempting to compare these poems with Wilfred Owen's. Wading through a sludge of consonants, the reader physically understands battle fatigue – not to mention the anger and irony of a man heartsick at old pieties about the ennobling qualities of war. Had Owen been a painter his palette would have been dark:

> Bent double, like old beggars under sacks,
> Knock-kneed, coughing like hags, we cursed through sludge,
> Till on the haunting flares we turned our backs
> And towards our distant rest began to trudge.

Apollinaire, though he was initially excited about the sights and sounds of war and its machinery, as he had been excited – like early Auden – about trains and planes, the machines of industrialization and travel (Apollinaire's brother Albert had moved to Mexico), would have shared many of Owen's experiences, even if, like his modernist painter friends, Apollinaire expressed himself in flights of fantasy, playfully and with vivid colours, softening his characteristic melancholy with humour – 'a most humorous sadness,' as Jacques says in *As You Like It*. Apollinaire, who could compare a bottle of champagne to a bomb, rarely lingers over his feelings of desolation but when he does, as in a poem-letter to his fiancée, Madeleine Pagès, the effect (see 'In the Cave-Shelter,' page 70) is devastating:

> . . . tonight I have a soul that feels hollow that feels empty
> As if one fell endlessly without ever touching the bottom
> Without a single thing to hang on to

In 'Wonder of War' (page 84) Apollinaire describes what Owen's 'Dulce et Decorum Est' calls 'the haunting flares':

> I feel as if I were a guest at some great feast lit up a giorno
> Earth is throwing herself a banquet
> Hungry she opens long pale mouths
> Earth is hungry and this is her cannibal Balthazar's feast
>
> Who'd have thought we could be such cannibals
> That it would take so much fire to roast the human body
> That's why the air has a slight acrid taste . . .

while one of his most quietly elegiac poems, 'Shadow' (page 40), finds simple words and images simply juxtaposed, not logically connected, to evoke dead comrades:

> Here you are at my side again
> Memories of my companions dead at war
> Olive of time
> Memories now all sewn into one
> As a hundred furs make only one coat
> As the thousands of wounds make only one newspaper
>   article . . .

Like Owen, Apollinaire died in 1918. Both were subversive of established attitudes, but Owen was a realist and Apollinaire, influenced by Cubism and by the Italian poet Marinetti's *Futurist Manifesto*, published in 1909, was more fanciful, more hyperbolic – 'magic' realist? Today the *Futurist Manifesto*'s aesthetic of violence can be linked to the rise of fascism (Marinetti would become a follower of Mussolini); at the time, however, the *Manifesto*'s celebration of 'the limits of logic', and new machinery ('. . . a roaring motor car which seems to run on machine-gun fire, is more beautiful than the Victory of Samothrace') inspired artistic movements across Europe. What Apollinaire experienced on the battlefield, as chronicled in his correspondence and in his poems, quickly gave him a more complex vision, marked by strange beauty, erotic yearnings and camaraderie, but also loneliness, fatigue, destruction and death.

By 1914, and the eve of war, Apollinaire was publishing his work – essays, poems – in journals and catalogues to art shows, among them the Georges Braque Exposition and a Robert Delaunay show for which he composed his wonderfully disjunctive 'conversation poem' 'Windows' (page 14). He was already the author of two collections of poems, *Bestiary* (1911) and *Alcools* (1913), with haunting Symbolist music. From *Alcools* Apollinaire had – a last-minute revision – deleted all punctuation, deciding that lineation and enjambment could do the job as well. That he was turning away from turn-of-the-century Symbolism towards something much more experimental is also evident in his long poem 'Zone' (page 2), which sets out as a stroll through the streets of Paris –

> Shepherdess O Eiffel Tower your herd of bridges is bleating
>   this morning

– and ranges in space-time from China to America and from Antiquity to the present. It was Apollinaire's manifesto for the poetic experiments he was to carry further in his 1918 volume *Calligrammes*, in which pronouns shift without warning, a fragmentation of the self that was inaugurated by Rimbaud's 1871 declaration that *je est un autre*. *Calligrammes* uses collage and juxtaposition, jump cuts, variable line lengths, and *calligrammes*, or 'beautiful writing', concrete poems (one is reproduced here) in which print is arranged so that the poems' visual aspect is as striking as the semantic – more than any other previous poet he raises the question of the relationship of words as such, when they appear on canvas, to image, and vice versa. Apollinaire's language, in *Calligrammes*, remains simple; he prefers plain diction and often childlike syntax ('Everything only connected by "and" and "and",' as Elizabeth Bishop was to write decades later in her poem 'Over 2,000 Illustrations and a Complete Concordance'); he avoids the preciosity and crystalline fixity of his Symbolist predecessor, Mallarmé; and in this 'naïveté' Apollinaire might be thought to resemble another of his painter friends, le Douanier Rousseau (who painted a double portrait of Apollinaire and Marie Laurencin), or, indeed, Picasso in many of his drawings and paintings. Before war broke out, Apollinaire hoped to collect these poetic experiments in a volume called 'Me Too I'm a Painter'. By the time he did publish them in a volume, he had added five more sections composed during the 'Grande Guerre'.

Apollinaire enlisted in December 1914. On his way to Nîmes in the south of France to join the 38th Artillery Regiment, he met a young school teacher, Madeleine Pagès, who became his friend, then fiancée and regular correspondent. Broken off in 1916, their love affair has left a trove of letters with poems and the raw material of poems written from Champagne-Ardennes, where Apollinaire had been posted, first in the artillery and then, at his request, in the infantry. In June 1915, at the front, he published a pamphlet containing the first group of war poems. Nine months later, in March 1916, days after being granted French nationality, Apollinaire was wounded in the head by shrapnel (his 'punctured helmet' is immortalized in 'Victory', page 106) and was evacuated, operated upon, and then transferred to Paris, where he was trepanned and, in June, awarded the Croix de Guerre. His last letter to Madeleine was in November 1916: 'My dear little Madeleine . . . I am tired . . . I am not what I was at all . . . I send you a thousand kisses.'

Assigned to office work in Paris, Apollinaire was promoted to the rank of lieutenant (acting). He took up his literary life again, but in November 1918, not fully recovered from his head wound, seven months after the publication of *Calligrammes* and his marriage to Jacqueline Kolb, to whom *Calligrammes'* last poem ('The Pretty Redhead,' page 114) is dedicated, Apollinaire caught Spanish flu and died. Paris was preparing to celebrate the Armistice: 'His funeral cortège followed the boulevard right to the Bastille and Père-Lachaise Cemetery through a crowd still delirious with joy,' his friend André Billy wrote.

*

This selection of Apollinaire's work includes a single poem – 'Zone' – from his 1913 collection *Alcools* and a selection from the six sections of *Calligrammes*. The poems in *Calligrammes'* first section ('Windows', 'Monday Rue Christine' and 'A Ghost of Clouds' here) are pre-war poems. The other five sections contain poems written between 1914 and 1918; they continue Apollinaire's experiments with language, and chronicle the war years. The second to last poem, 'Victory', looks forward to the artistic challenges of the post-war period –

> Oh mouths men are seeking a new language
> Which no grammarian of any language will find fault with
>
> And these old languages are so close to death
> Truly it's out of habit and for lack of daring
> That we still use them for poetry
> [. . .]
> Let's have new sounds new sounds new sounds

– a call to action that would be taken up by Apollinaire's poet friend André Breton, author of the 1924 *Surrealist Manifesto*, and by other members of the postwar avant-garde that Apollinaire did so much to inspire.

Particular questions of translation, and the circumstances surrounding the poems' composition, where available, will be found in the translator's notes at the end of the volume. I have tried to respect Apollinaire's preference for the plain word ('look', for example, rather than the more recherché 'gaze'); and his use of juxtaposition and simple grammatical constructions over more elaborate ones; and the contents of each, often expansive line, and the order in which ideas are expressed. Apollinaire was writing much more free verse now, but he was always a deft user of rhyme; I have tried to suggest, where poems in this selection are rhymed, his use of rhyme, as, for example, in the humorous couplet rhymes of 'Zone' and 'In Nîmes'. His poetics reflected his desire to capture the world in all its fleetingness, complexity, and simultaneity of time and space, with an almost childlike fresh-ness, creating out of the street scenes of early twentieth-century Paris and the often bleak and always dangerous circumstances of day-to-day life in the trenches a world at once magical, full of eros and melancholy:

> Looking through the open entrance of the trench carved
>   out of chalk
> Towards the far wall that looks as if it were made of nougat

says 'The Thunder's Palace' (page 60), a detailed description of a dugout that concludes with a profession of faith in simplicity and patina:

> And whatever is burdened with ornament
> Needs to age to acquire the beauty one calls ancient
> And which is the nobility the force the ardour the soul
>   the lustre
> Of what is new and what is useful
> Especially if it is plain and simple
> As plain and simple as the thunder's small palace

Apollinaire's poems are themselves small palaces of thunder.

BEVERLEY BIE BRAHIC

GUILLAUME APOLLINAIRE

The Little Auto

Zone

A la fin tu es las de ce monde ancien

Bergère ô tour Eiffel le troupeau des ponts bêle ce matin

Tu en as assez de vivre dans l'antiquité grecque et romaine

Ici même les automobiles ont l'air d'être anciennes
La religion seule est restée toute neuve la religion
Est restée simple comme les hangars de Port-Aviation

Seul en Europe tu n'es pas antique ô Christianisme
L'Européen le plus moderne c'est vous Pape Pie X
Et toi que les fenêtres observent la honte te retient
D'entrer dans une église et de t'y confesser ce matin
Tu lis les prospectus les catalogues les affiches qui chantent tout
    haut
Voilà la poésie ce matin et pour la prose il y a les journaux
Il y a les livraisons à 25 centimes pleines d'aventures policières
Portraits des grands hommes et mille titres divers

J'ai vu ce matin une jolie rue dont j'ai oublié le nom
Neuve et propre du soleil elle était le clairon
Les directeurs les ouvriers et les belles sténo-dactylographes
Du lundi matin au samedi soir quatre fois par jour y passent
Le matin par trois fois la sirène y gémit
Une cloche rageuse y aboie vers midi
Les inscriptions des enseignes et des murailles
Les plaques les avis à la façon des perroquets criaillent

Zone

In the end you're tired of this old world

Shepherdess O Eiffel Tower your herd of bridges is bleating this
    morning

You've had enough of living with Greek and Roman antiques

Here even the automobiles look like relics
Only religion is still brand new religion
Remains as simple as the hangars at Port-Aviation

In Europe you alone are not antique O Christianity
The most modern European is you Pope Pius X
And you whom the windows are watching shame keeps you
    from stepping
Into a church for confession this morning
You read the flyers the catalogues and the posters that sing at the
    top of their lungs
There's poetry for you this morning and for prose you've got
    newspapers
25 cents apiece with plenty of crimes
Profiles of the great and a zillion different headlines

This morning I saw a pretty street whose name I've forgotten
Bright and shining fanfare for the sun
Managers workers and beautiful typists
Monday through Saturday four times a day they go past
In the morning three times the siren wails
Towards noon the crazy yapping of the bells
On shop signs and walls on nameplates
On notices the lettering squawks like parrots

J'aime la grâce de cette rue industrielle
Située à Paris entre la rue Aumont-Thiéville et l'avenue des
    Ternes

Voilà la jeune rue et tu n'es encore qu'un petit enfant
Ta mère ne t'habille que de bleu et de blanc
Tu es très pieux et avec le plus ancien de tes camarades René
    Dalize
Vous n'aimez rien tant que les pompes de l'Église
Il est neuf heures le gaz est baissé tout bleu vous sortez du
    dortoir en cachette
Vous priez toute la nuit dans la chapelle du collège
Tandis qu'éternelle et adorable profondeur améthyste
Tourne à jamais la flamboyante gloire du Christ
C'est le beau lys que tous nous cultivons
C'est la torche aux cheveux roux que n'éteint pas le vent
C'est le fils pâle et vermeil de la douloureuse mère
C'est l'arbre toujours touffu de toutes les prières
C'est la double potence de l'honneur et de l'éternité
C'est l'étoile à six branches
C'est Dieu qui meurt le vendredi et ressuscite le dimanche
C'est le Christ qui monte au ciel mieux que les aviateurs
Il détient le record du monde pour la hauteur

Pupille Christ de l'œil
Vingtième pupille des siècles il sait y faire
Et changé en oiseau ce siècle comme Jésus monte dans l'air
Les diables dans les abîmes lèvent la tête pour le regarder
Ils disent qu'il imite Simon Mage en Judée
Ils crient s'il sait voler qu'on l'appelle voleur
Les anges voltigent autour du joli voltigeur
Icare Enoch Elie Apollonius de Thyane
Flottent autour du premier aéroplane
Ils s'écartent parfois pour laisser passer ceux que transporte la
    Sainte-Eucharistie

I love the charm of this industrial street
Located in Paris between Aumont-Thiéville Street and the
    Avenue des Ternes

Here's the young street and you are a child still
Your mother dresses you in blue and white still
You are very religious and for you and your best friend René
    Dalize
The Church's pomp is as good as it gets
It's nine o'clock the gas is turned low in blue you sneak out of the
    dormitory
All night long in the school chapel you pray
While eternal and adorable shadows of amethyst
Flicker forever the flamboyant glory of Christ
This is the beautiful lily we all want to cultivate
This is the red-haired torch no wind can blow out
This is the pale vermilion son of a sorrowing mother
This is the evergreen tree of all prayer
This is the double gallows of honour forever and ever
This is the star with six points
This is God who dies on Friday and on Sunday resuscitates
This is Christ who flies to heaven better than any aviator
He holds the world record for height

Pupil Christ of the eye
Twentieth pupil of the centuries he has the savoir-faire
And changed to a bird this century as Jesus climbs in the air
In the depths the devils crane their necks to stare
He thinks he's Simon Magus in Judea they mutter
If he's so smart they shout why doesn't he scat
Angels swoop around the pretty acrobat
Icarus Enoch Elijah Apollonius of Tyana
Hover over the very first airplane
Sometimes they make room for the Holy Eucharist

Ces prêtres qui montent éternellement élevant l'hostie
L'avion se pose enfin sans refermer les ailes
Le ciel s'emplit alors de millions d'hirondelles
A tire-d'aile viennent les corbeaux les faucons les hiboux
D'Afrique arrivent les ibis les flamants les marabouts
L'oiseau Roc célébré par les conteurs et les poètes
Plane tenant dans les serres le crâne d'Adam la première tête
L'aigle fond de l'horizon en poussant un grand cri
Et d'Amérique vient le petit colibri
De Chine sont venus les pihis longs et souples
Qui n'ont qu'une seule aile et qui volent par couples
Puis voici la colombe esprit immaculé
Qu'escortent l'oiseau-lyre et le paon ocellé
Le phénix ce bûcher qui soi-même s'engendre
Un instant voile tout de son ardente cendre
Les sirènes laissant les périlleux détroits
Arrivent en chantant bellement toutes trois
Et tous aigle phénix et pihis de la Chine
Fraternisent avec la volante machine

Maintenant tu marches dans Paris tout seul parmi la foule
Des troupeaux d'autobus mugissants près de toi roulent
L'angoisse de l'amour te serre le gosier
Comme si tu ne devais jamais plus être aimé
Si tu vivais dans l'ancien temps tu entrerais dans un monastère
Vous avez honte quand vous vous surprenez à dire une prière
Tu te moques de toi et comme le feu de l'Enfer ton rire pétille
Les étincelles de ton rire dorent le fond de ta vie
C'est un tableau pendu dans un sombre musée
Et quelquefois tu vas le regarder de près

Aujourd'hui tu marches dans Paris les femmes sont
    ensanglantées
C'était et je voudrais ne pas m'en souvenir c'était au déclin de la
    beauté

Priests endlessly elevating with the Host
Wings still outspread the airplane touches down
As millions of swallows fill the heavens
The falcons come winging owls and crows
From Africa ibises marabous and flamingos
The roc bird celebrated by poets and spinners of tales
Hovers gripping the first head Adam's skull
From the horizon with a shriek the eagle falls
And from America the tiny colibri with its trills
From China the pihis turn up long and supple
They each have one wing and fly in couples
Along comes the dove that spotless soul
Escorted by the lyre-bird and that eye-full
The peacock the phoenix a self-engendering pyre
One instant veils all its ashen fire
The Sirens say goodbye to their perilous Narrows
And come along singing melodious trios
And all of them the eagle phoenix and Chinese
Pihis fraternize with the incredible flying machine

Now you walk in Paris all alone in the crowd
Beside you lowing buses sway like cattle in a herd
Love-sickness makes a lump in your throat
As if you were never again to be loved
Once you would have entered a cloister
You're embarrassed to catch yourself mouthing a prayer
You laugh at yourself and your laughter sparkles like hellfire
The sparks of your laughter make life's dregs glitter
It's a painting hung in museum darkness
And sometimes you go to see it up close

Today you walk in Paris the women are bloody
This was I wish I could forget this was the beginning of the end
    of beauty

Entourée de flammes ferventes Notre-Dame m'a regardé à
    Chartres
Le sang de votre Sacré-Cœur m'a inondé à Montmartre
Je suis malade d'ouïr les paroles bienheureuses
L'amour dont je souffre est une maladie honteuse
Et l'image qui te possède te fait survivre dans l'insomnie et dans
    l'angoisse
C'est toujours près de toi cette image qui passe

Maintenant tu es au bord de la Méditerranée
Sous les citronniers qui sont en fleur toute l'année
Avec tes amis tu te promènes en barque
L'un est Nissard il y a un Mentonasque et deux Turbiasques
Nous regardons avec effroi les poulpes des profondeurs
Et parmi les algues nagent les poissons images du Sauveur

Tu es dans le jardin d'une auberge aux environs de Prague
Tu te sens tout heureux une rose est sur la table
Et tu observes au lieu d'écrire ton conte en prose
La cétoine qui dort dans le cœur de la rose

Épouvanté tu te vois dessiné dans les agates de Saint-Vit
Tu étais triste à mourir le jour où tu t'y vis
Tu ressembles au Lazare affolé par le jour
Les aiguilles de l'horloge du quartier juif vont à rebours
Et tu recules aussi dans ta vie lentement
En montant au Hradchin et le soir en écoutant
Dans les tavernes chanter des chansons tchèques

Te voici à Marseille au milieu des pastèques

Te voici à Coblence à l'hôtel du Géant

Te voici à Rome assis sous un néflier du Japon

From fervent flames Our Lady gazed at me at Chartres
The blood of your Sacred Heart washed over me in Montmartre
Hearing the blissful words I feel ill
My love is a sickness and shameful
This image you possess sustains you through insomnia and
    anxiety
This image stays with you always

Now you are on the edge of the Mediterranean
The lemon trees here are always in bloom
With your friends you go for a sail on the sea
One's from Nice one from Menton and two from La Turbie
The tentacles of the deep fill us with fear
In the seaweeds swim fishes in the image of Our Saviour

You are in the garden of an inn near Prague
You feel so happy there's rose on the table
And you observe instead of writing your tale in prose
The beetle that sleeps in the heart of the rose

Terrified you see yourself in the agates of Saint Vitus
That day you could have died of sadness
You look like Lazarus dazed by daylight
In the Jewish quarter the clock's hands go from right
To left and you too go slowly backwards in life
Climbing to Hradchin and listening each night
In the taverns to people singing Czech songs

Here you are in Marseille surrounded by watermelons

Here you are in Coblenz in the Hotel of the Giant

Here you are in Rome sitting under a Japanese loquat

Te voici à Amsterdam avec une jeune fille que tu trouves belle et
    qui est laide
Elle doit se marier avec un étudiant de Leyde
On y loue des chambres en latin Cubicula locanda
Je m'en souviens j'y ai passé trois jours et autant à Gouda

Tu es à Paris chez le juge d'instruction
Comme un criminel on te met en état d'arrestation

Tu as fait de douloureux et de joyeux voyages
Avant de t'apercevoir du mensonge et de l'âge
Tu as souffert de l'amour à vingt et à trente ans
J'ai vécu comme un fou et j'ai perdu mon temps
Tu n'oses plus regarder tes mains et à tous moments je voudrais
    sangloter
Sur toi sur celle que j'aime sur tout ce qui t'a épouvanté

Tu regardes les yeux pleins de larmes ces pauvres émigrants
Ils croient en Dieu ils prient les femmes allaitent des enfants
Ils emplissent de leur odeur le hall de la gare Saint-Lazare
Ils ont foi dans leur étoile comme les rois-mages
Ils espèrent gagner de l'argent dans l'Argentine
Et revenir dans leur pays après avoir fait fortune
Une famille transporte un édredon rouge comme vous
    transportez votre cœur
Cet édredon et nos rêves sont aussi irréels
Quelques-uns de ces émigrants restent ici et se logent
Rue des Rosiers ou rue des Écouffes dans des bouges
Je les ai vus souvent le soir ils prennent l'air dans la rue
Et se déplacent rarement comme les pièces aux échecs
Il y a surtout des Juifs leurs femmes portent perruque
Elles restent assises exsangues au fond des boutiques

Tu es debout devant le zinc d'un bar crapuleux
Tu prends un café à deux sous parmi les malheureux

Here you are in Amsterdam with a girl you find beautiful and
    who's ugly
There's a student from Leyden she's engaged to marry
Up there one rents rooms in Latin Cubicula locanda
I remember three days there and about the same in Gouda

In Paris the judge sentences you without bail
Like a common criminal they throw you in jail

You went on some painful and some joyous voyages
Before you wised up to liars and age
Lovesick at twenty at thirty a basket case still
I've wasted my time and I've lived like a fool
You're afraid to look at your hands now and all the time I feel
    like bursting into tears
About you about the girl I love about all of my fears

With tears in your eyes you look at these poor emigrants
They believe in God they pray the women nurse infants
Their smell wafts through the Gare Saint-Lazare
Like the Wise Men they follow their star
They hope to strike it rich in the Argentine
And come back home having made a fortune
One family transports a red comforter the way you transport
    your heart
Their comforter and our dreams are equally unreal
Some emigrants settle here and share rooms
Rue des Rosiers or Rue des Écouffes in the slums
In the evening getting a breath of air in the street I see them
Standing around like pawns in a chess game
Mostly they're Jews their wives wear wigs
And sit like lumps in the backs of the shops

At the bar of some dive you are one of the lost
Drinking coffee at two cents a shot

Tu es la nuit dans un grand restaurant

Ces femmes ne sont pas méchantes elles ont des soucis cependant
Toutes même la plus laide a fait souffrir son amant

Elle est la fille d'un sergent de ville de Jersey

Ses mains que je n'avais pas vues sont dures et gercées

J'ai une pitié immense pour les coutures de son ventre

J'humilie maintenant à une pauvre fille au rire horrible ma
    bouche

Tu es seul le matin va venir
Les laitiers font tinter leurs bidons dans les rues

La nuit s'éloigne ainsi qu'une belle Métive
C'est Ferdine la fausse ou Léa l'attentive

Et tu bois cet alcool brûlant comme ta vie
Ta vie que tu bois comme une eau-de-vie

Tu marches vers Auteuil tu veux aller chez toi à pied
Dormir parmi tes fétiches d'Océanie et de Guinée
Ils sont des Christ d'une autre forme et d'une autre croyance
Ce sont les Christ inférieurs des obscures espérances

Adieu Adieu

Soleil cou coupé

Night finds you in a fancy restaurant

Those women aren't all that bad they have problems however
All of them even the ugliest has made her lover suffer

She's the daughter of Jersey police officer

Her hands I hadn't seen are chapped and hard

I feel such pity for her belly's scars

Now I humble my mouth to a poor girl with a god-awful laugh

You are alone morning is coming
Milkmen jingle their cans in the street

Like a dark beauty the night retires
Kindly Lea or Ferdine who's a liar

And you drink this alcohol that flames like your life
Your life you toss back like a shot of brandy

You want to go home on foot you walk towards Auteuil
You want to sleep with your fetishes from Polynesia or Guinea
Other Christs with other beliefs
Lesser Christs repositories of obscure faiths

Adieu Adieu

Sun neck cut

Les Fenêtres

Du rouge au vert tout le jaune se meurt
Quand chantent les aras dans les forêts natales
Abatis de pihis
Il y a un poème à faire sur l'oiseau qui n'a qu'une aile
Nous l'enverrons en message téléphonique
Traumatisme géant
Il fait couler les yeux
Voilà une jolie jeune fille parmi les jeunes Turinaises
Le pauvre jeune homme se mouchait dans sa cravate blanche
Tu soulèveras le rideau
Et maintenant voilà que s'ouvre la fenêtre
Araignées quand les mains tissaient la lumière
Beauté pâleur insondables violets
Nous tenterons en vain de prendre du repos
On commencera à minuit
Quand on a le temps on a la liberté
Bigorneaux Lotte multiples Soleils et l'Oursin du couchant
Une vieille paire de chaussures jaunes devant la fenêtre
Tours
Les Tours ce sont les rues
Puits
Puits ce sont les places
Puits
Arbres creux qui abritent les Câpresses vagabondes
Les Chabins chantent des airs à mourir
Aux Chabines marronnes
Et l'oie oua-oua trompette au nord
Où les chasseurs de ratons
Raclent les pelleteries
Étincelant diamant

Windows

From red to green all the yellow dies
When the parrots sing in their native forests
Pihi massacre
There's a poem in the bird with only one wing
We'll send it along in a telephone message
Giant traumatism
It makes your eyes run
Now there's a pretty girl among the girls from Turin
That poor young man was blowing his nose into his white
    necktie
You will lift the curtain
And now see how the window opens
Spiders when hands wove the light
Beauty paleness unfathomable violets
One will try and try to get some rest
We will start at midnight
When one has the time one has the freedom
Winkles Whitefish multiple Suns and the Sea Urchin of sundown
An old pair of yellow shoes in front of the window
Towers
Towers are streets
Wells
Wells are squares
Wells
Hollow trees to shelter the wandering Caperesses
The Chabins sing songs to die for
To the maroon Chabinesses
And the goose honk-honks on its horn up north
Where the muskrat hunters
Scrape skins
Glittering diamond

Vancouver
Où le train blanc de neige et de feux nocturnes fuit l'hiver
O Paris
Du rouge au vert tout le jaune se meurt
Paris Vancouver Hyères Maintenon New-York et les Antilles
La fenêtre s'ouvre comme une orange
Le beau fruit de la lumière

Vancouver
Where the train white with snow and night's fires flees winter
O Paris
From red to green all the yellow dies
Paris Vancouver Hyères Maintenon New York and the Antilles
The window opens like an orange
Lovely fruit of the light

Lundi Rue Christine

La mère de la concierge et la concierge laisseront tout passer
Si tu es un homme tu m'accompagneras ce soir
Il suffirait qu'un type maintînt la porte cochère
Pendant que l'autre monterait

Trois becs de gaz allumés
La patronne est poitrinaire
Quand tu auras fini nous jouerons une partie de jacquet
Un chef d'orchestre qui a mal à la gorge
Quand tu viendras à Tunis je te ferai fumer du kief

Ça a l'air de rimer

Des piles de soucoupes des fleurs un calendrier
Pim pam pim
Je dois fiche près de 300 francs à ma probloque
Je préférerais me couper le parfaitement que de les lui donner.

Je partirai à 20 h. 27
Six glaces s'y dévisagent toujours
Je crois que nous allons nous embrouiller encore davantage

Cher monsieur
Vous êtes un mec à la mie de pain
Cette dame a le nez comme un ver solitaire
Louise a oublié sa fourrure
Moi je n'ai pas de fourrure et je n'ai pas froid
Le Danois fume sa cigarette en consultant l'horaire
Le chat noir traverse la brasserie

Monday Rue Christine

The concierge and her mother will let anyone in
If you're a man you'll come with me tonight
All it takes is one of us to keep the porte cochère open
While the other goes up

Three gas lamps lit
The proprietress is wasting away
When you're done we'll play backgammon
An orchestra conductor who has a sore throat
When you come to Tunis we'll smoke hashish

That seems to add up

Stack of saucers some flowers a calendar
Bling bang bling
I owe my landlord nearly 300 fucking francs
I'd as soon chop it off as give her the money

I'm leaving at 8:27 p.m.
Six mirrors still staring at each other over there
I think we're going to get ourselves into a real fix

Dear sir
You're a wimp
That lady has the nose of a tapeworm
Louise forgot her fur
Well I haven't any fur and I'm not cold
The Danish guy's smoking his cigarette and studying the
    schedule
The black cat crosses the brasserie

Ces crêpes étaient exquises
La fontaine coule
Robe noire comme ses ongles
C'est complètement impossible
Voici monsieur
La bague en malachite
Le sol est semé de sciure
Alors c'est vrai
La serveuse rousse a été enlevée par un libraire

Un journaliste que je connais d'ailleurs très vaguement

Écoute Jacques c'est très sérieux ce que je vais te dire

Compagnie de navigation mixte

Il me dit monsieur voulez-vous voir ce que je peux faire d'eaux
	fortes et de tableaux
Je n'ai qu'une petite bonne

Après déjeuner café du Luxembourg

Une fois là il me présente un gros bonhomme
Qui me dit
Écoutez c'est charmant
A Smyrne à Naples en Tunisie
Mais nom de Dieu où est-ce
La dernière fois que j'ai été en Chine
C'est il y a huit ou neuf ans
L'Honneur tient souvent à l'heure que marque la pendule
La quinte major

Those crêpes were delicious
The fountain's dripping
Dress black as her nails
It's totally out of the question
Here you are sir
The malachite ring
The floor is littered with sawdust
So it's true
The red-haired waitress has been nabbed by a bookseller

A journalist whom as a matter of fact I know vaguely

Listen Jacques what I'm about to say is extremely serious

Mixed Navigation Company Ltd

So he says sir would you like me to show you my etchings and
    paintings
All I have is one little housemaid

After lunch at the Café de Luxembourg

When I get there he introduces me to this football-player type
Who tells me
Listen you're going to love this
In Smyrna in Naples in Tunisia
Oh for godssake where is it
The last time I was in China
Eight or nine years ago that was
Honour is often a matter of what o'clock it is
Royal flush

Un Fantôme De Nuées

Comme c'était la veille du quatorze juillet
Vers les quatre heures de l'après-midi
Je descendis dans la rue pour aller voir les saltimbanques

Ces gens qui font des tours en plein air
Commencent à être rares à Paris
Dans ma jeunesse on en voyait beaucoup plus qu'aujourd'hui
Ils s'en sont allés presque tous en province

Je pris le boulevard Saint-Germain
Et sur une petite place située entre Saint-Germain-des-Prés et la
    statue de Danton
Je rencontrai les saltimbanques

La foule les entourait muette et résignée à attendre
Je me fis une place dans ce cercle afin de tout voir
Poids formidables
Villes de Belgique soulevées à bras tendu par un ouvrier russe de
    Longwy
Haltères noirs et creux qui ont pour tige un fleuve figé
Doigts roulant une cigarette amère et délicieuse comme la vie

De nombreux tapis sales couvraient le sol
Tapis qui ont des plis qu'on ne défera pas
Tapis qui sont presque entièrement couleur de la poussière
Et où quelques taches jaunes ou vertes ont persisté
Comme un air de musique qui vous poursuit

Vois-tu le personnage maigre et sauvage
La cendre de ses pères lui sortait en barbe grisonnante
Il portait ainsi toute son hérédité au visage

A Ghost of Clouds

Since it was the eve of the Fourteenth of July
At about four o'clock in the afternoon
I went out in the streets to see the saltimbancos

Those street artists
Are becoming rare in Paris
In my youth you'd see a lot more of them
Nowadays they've mostly moved to the provinces

I took the Boulevard Saint-Germain
And on a little square between Saint-Germain-des-Prés and
    Danton's statue
I found the saltimbancos

People crowded round them silent and resigned to waiting
I squeezed into the circle where I could see everything
Amazing weights
Whole Belgian cities raised on the outstretched arm of a Russian
    worker from Longwy
Hollow black dumb-bells whose bar is a frozen river
Fingers rolling a cigarette bitter and delicious as life

Filthy rugs covered the ground
Carpets with wrinkles you'll never smooth out
Carpets more or less the colour of dust
With here and there a patch of green or yellow
Like a tune you cannot stop singing.

See that skinny wild-looking character
His forefathers' ashes were coming out in a grizzled beard
The whole burden of his heredity was inscribed in his face

Il semblait rêver à l'avenir
En tournant machinalement un orgue de Barbarie
Dont la lente voix se lamentait merveilleusement
Les glouglous les couacs et les sourds gémissements

Les saltimbanques ne bougeaient pas
Le plus vieux avait un maillot couleur de ce rose violâtre qu'ont
    aux joues certaines jeunes filles fraîches mais près de la mort

Ce rose-là se niche surtout dans les plis qui entourent souvent
    leur bouche
Ou près des narines
C'est un rose plein de traîtrise

Cet homme portait-il ainsi sur le dos
La teinte ignoble de ses poumons

Les bras les bras partout montaient la garde

Le second saltimbanque
N'était vêtu que de son ombre
Je le regardai longtemps
Son visage m'échappe entièrement
C'est un homme sans tête

Un autre enfin avait l'air d'un voyou
D'un apache bon et crapule à la fois
Avec son pantalon bouffant et les accroche-chaussettes
N'aurait-il pas eu l'apparence d'un maquereau à sa toilette

La musique se tut et ce furent des pourparlers avec le public
Qui sou à sou jeta sur le tapis la somme de deux francs cinquante
Au lieu des trois francs que le vieux avait fixés comme prix des
    tours

He seemed to be dreaming about the future
As he cranked a Barbary organ
Whose slow voice lamented marvellously
The gurgles the squawks and dull moans

The saltimbancos didn't budge
The oldest wore a shirt that rose-violet colour you see in the cheeks
    of certain girls who look blooming but are close to death

That rose nestles into the folds they often have around their
    mouths
Or near their nostrils
It's a rose you can't trust

In the same way that man wore
The vile colour of his lungs on his back

The arms the arms everywhere stood guard

The second saltimbanco
Wore only his shadow
I looked at him for a long time
His face utterly escapes me
He is a man without a head

Another one looked like a thug
A soft touch but a crook
With his baggy trousers and his socks and his garters
He looked like a pimp dolled up for a night on the town

The music stopped and it was time to chat up the crowd
Which penny by penny tossed the sum of two francs fifty down
    on the rug
Instead of the three francs the old man said was the price for the
    show

Mais quand il fut clair que personne ne donnerait plus rien
On se décida à commencer la séance
De dessous l'orgue sortit un tout petit saltimbanque habillé de
    rose pulmonaire
Avec de la fourrure aux poignets et aux chevilles
Il poussait des cris brefs
Et saluait en écartant gentiment les avant-bras
Mains ouvertes

Une jambe en arrière prête à la génuflexion
Il salua ainsi aux quatre points cardinaux
Et quand il marcha sur une boule
Son corps mince devint une musique si délicate que nul parmi
    les spectateurs n'y fut insensible
Un petit esprit sans aucune humanité
Pensa chacun
Et cette musique des formes
Détruisit celle de l'orgue mécanique
Que moulait l'homme au visage couvert d'ancêtres

Le petit saltimbanque fit la roue
Avec tant d'harmonie
Que l'orgue cessa de jouer
Et que l'organiste se cacha le visage dans les mains
Aux doigts semblables aux descendants de son destin
Fœtus minuscules qui lui sortaient de la barbe
Nouveaux cris de Peau-Rouge
Musique angélique des arbres
Disparition de l'enfant
Les saltimbanques soulevèrent les gros haltères à bout de bras
Ils jonglèrent avec les poids

Mais chaque spectateur cherchait en soi l'enfant miraculeux
Siècle ô siècle des nuages

When it was obvious no one was going to cough up another cent
They decided to start the show
Out from under the organ popped a tiny little saltimbanco
    dressed in a consumptive pink
With fur at the cuffs of his wrists and ankles
He uttered some war cries
And bowed by holding his arms out nicely
With the palms turned up

One leg behind as if to genuflect
He bowed to the four cardinal points
And when he balanced on a ball
His thin body made such delicate music not one spectator
    remained unmoved
A sprite without a speck of humanity
Each was thinking
And this shapely music
Destroyed the music of the mechanical organ
That the man was grinding out whose face crawled with ancestors

The little saltimbanco did a cartwheel
With such grace
The organ stopped playing
And the organist hid his face in his hands
Whose fingers seemed like his descendants' destiny
Tiny foetuses creeping from his beard
More Redskin yelps
Angelic music of the trees
Disappearance of the child
Arms outstretched the saltimbancos raised the great dumb-bells
They juggled with the weights

But each spectator was searching within himself for the
    miraculous child
Century oh century of clouds

La Petite Auto

Le 31 du mois d'Août 1914
Je partis de Deauville un peu avant minuit
Dans la petite auto de Rouveyre

Avec son chauffeur nous étions trois

Nous dîmes adieu à toute une époque
Des géants furieux se dressaient sur l'Europe
Les aigles quittaient leur aire attendant le soleil
Les poissons voraces montaient des abîmes
Les peuples accouraient pour se connaître à fond
Les morts tremblaient de peur dans leurs sombres demeures

Les chiens aboyaient vers là-bas où étaient les frontières
Je m'en allais portant en moi toutes ces armées qui se battaient
Je les sentais monter en moi et s'étaler les contrées où elles
    serpentaient
Avec les forêts les villages heureux de la Belgique
Francorchamps avec l'Eau Rouge et les pouhons
Région par où se font toujours les invasions
Artères ferroviaires où ceux qui s'en allaient mourir
Saluaient encore une fois la vie colorée
Océans profonds où remuaient les monstres
Dans les vieilles carcasses naufragées
Hauteurs inimaginables où l'homme combat
Plus haut que l'aigle ne plane
L'homme y combat contre l'homme
Et descend tout à coup comme une étoile filante
Je sentais en moi des êtres neufs pleins de dextérité

The Little Auto

On the 31st of the month of August 1914
I left Deauville not long before midnight
In Rouveyre's little auto

Counting his chauffeur there were three of us

We bid farewell to a whole era
Furious giants were rising up over Europe
Eagles were leaving their aeries waiting for the sun
Voracious fish were swimming up from the abysses
Peoples came running to get to know one another better
The dead were shaking with fear in their dark dwellings

Dogs were barking over where the borders were
I left carrying with me inside me all those armies that were
     fighting
I could feel them rising inside me and rolling out the lands their
     columns were snaking through
With the orests the happy villages of Belgium
Francorchamps with Eau Rouge the Red River and the pouhons
     springs
The region the invasions have always passed through
Railroad arteries where those who were marching off to die
Saluted life's colours one last time
Deep oceans where monsters were shuddering
Among the ancient shipwreck carcasses
Unimaginable heights where man fights
Higher than the eagle can soar
Man fights man up there
And falls without warning like a shooting star
Inside me I could feel some dexterous new beings

Bâtir et aussi agencer un univers nouveau
Un marchand d'une opulence inouïe et d'une taille prodigieuse
Disposait un étalage extraordinaire
Et des bergers gigantesques menaient
De grands troupeaux muets qui broutaient les paroles
Et contre lesquels aboyaient tous les chiens sur la route

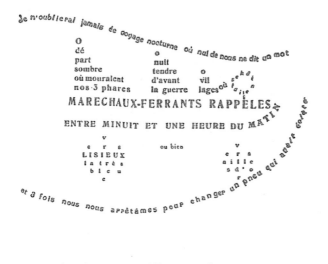

Et quand après avoir passé l'après-midi

Par Fontainebleau

Nous arrivâmes à Paris

Au moment où l'on affichait la mobilisation

Nous comprîmes mon camarade et moi

Que la petite auto nous avait conduits dans une époque Nouvelle

Et bien qu'étant déjà tous deux des hommes mûrs

Nous venions cependant de naître

Building and also furnishing a new universe
A merchant of unbelievable opulence and prodigious size
Was setting out his fabulous wares
And gigantic shepherds were leading
Huge dumb flocks that were grazing on the speeches
And along the road all the dogs were barking at them

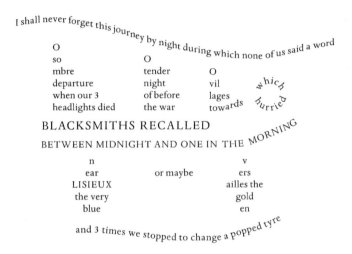

I shall never forget this journey by night during which none of us said a word

        O
    so   O
    mbre   tender   O
    departure   night   vil   which
    when our 3 of before   lages   hurried
    headlights died the war   towards

BLACKSMITHS RECALLED

BETWEEN MIDNIGHT AND ONE IN THE MORNING

        n   v
        ear   or maybe   ers
        LISIEUX   ailles the
        the very   gold
        blue   en

        and 3 times we stopped to change a popped tyre

And when after having passed that afternoon
Through Fontainebleau
We arrived in Paris
Just as they were posting the mobilization orders
We understood my comrade and I
That the little auto had driven us into a New Era
And although we were both already grown men
We had just been born

Fumées

Et tandis que la guerre
Ensanglante la terre
Je hausse les odeurs
Près des couleurs-saveurs

Et je fu
m
e
du
ta
bac
de
zoNE

Des fleurs à ras du sol regardent par bouffées
Les boucles des odeurs par tes mains décoiffées
Mais je connais aussi les grottes parfumées
Où gravite l'azur unique des fumées
Où plus doux que la nuit et plus pur que le jour
Tu t'étends comme un dieu fatigué par l'amour
Tu fascines les flammes
Elles rampent à tes pieds
Ces nonchalantes femmes
Tes feuilles de papier

Up in Smoke

And while the war cry
Turns the earth bloody
I hoist the odours
Beside the colour-savours

    And I sm
        o
         ke
         the
         to
         bac
          co
         of
        the ZoNE

Ground-hugging flowers look at the circles
The ringlets of odours your hands dishevel
But I know also the perfumed dens
Where the smoke's rare blue gravitates and settles
Where sweeter than night and purer than day then
You sprawl like a god exhausted by love
      You fascinate the flames
      They crawl at your feet
      Those nonchalant women
      Your paper sheets

À Nîmes

A Émile Léonard

Je me suis engagé sous le plus beau des cieux
Dans Nice la Marine au nom victorieux

Perdu parmi 900 conducteurs anonymes
Je suis un charretier du neuf charroi de Nîmes

L'Amour dit Reste ici Mais là-bas les obus
Épousent ardemment et sans cesse les buts

J'attends que le printemps commande que s'en aille
Vers le nord glorieux l'intrépide bleusaille

Les 3 servants assis dodelinent leurs fronts
Où brillent leurs yeux clairs comme mes éperons

Un bel après-midi de garde à l'écurie
J'entends sonner les trompettes d'artillerie

J'admire la gaieté de ce détachement
Qui va rejoindre au front notre beau régiment

Le territorial se mange une salade
A l'anchois en parlant de sa femme malade

4 pointeurs fixaient les bulles des niveaux
Qui remuaient ainsi que les yeux des chevaux

Le bon chanteur Girault nous chante après 9 heures
Un grand air d'opéra toi l'écoutant tu pleures

In Nîmes

for Émile Léonard

I've enlisted under skies so glorious
In Maritime Nice its name victorious

One of 900 anonymous drivers
In Nîmes Ninth Convoy I am a carter

Love says Stay here But up there the shells
Ceaselessly ardently espouse their goals

I'm waiting for spring to come and order
The valiant recruits to the great north border

Heads nodding sit the 3 gunners
Their grey eyes glint like my spurs

A fine afternoon on guard at the stable
I can hear the artillery's horns tootle

I admire the gaiety of this detachment
At the front it will join our fine regiment

The territorial nibbles on a leaf
Of anchovy salad and talks about his sick wife

4 gun layers fix levels whose bubbles
Were as shifty as the horses' eyeballs

After dinner Girault the great singer will sing
Grand old opera tunes you weep listening

Je flatte de la main le petit canon gris
Gris comme l'eau de Seine et je songe à Paris

Mais ce pâle blessé m'a dit à la cantine
Des obus dans la nuit la splendeur argentine

Je mâche lentement ma portion de bœuf
Je me promène seul le soir de 5 à 9

Je selle mon cheval nous battons la campagne
Je te salue au loin belle rose ô tour Magne

My hand strokes the little grey cannon
Grey like the Seine and of Paris I dream

But in the canteen a whey-faced casualty
Told me shells at night are splendid and silvery

Slowly I munch on my ration of beef
I walk alone from 5 to 9 each evening

I saddle my horse and the back roads are ours
Lovely rose O Tour Magne I salute you from afar

Veille

Mon cher André Rouveyre
Troudla la Champignon Tabatière
On ne sait quand on partira
Ni quand on reviendra

Au Mercure de France
Mars revient tout couleur d'espérance
J'ai envoyé mon papier
Sur papier quadrillé

J'entends les pas des grands chevaux d'artillerie allant au trot sur
    la grand-route où moi je veille
Un grand manteau gris de crayon comme le ciel m'enveloppe
    jusqu'à l'oreille

        Quel
        Ciel
        Triste
        Piste
        Où
        Vale
        Pâle
        Sou-
        rire
De la lune qui me regarde éctire

Night Watch

My dear André Rouveyre
Troudla la Champignon Tabatière
Who knows when we go
Or when we come back-o

In the Mercure de France
March comes back the colour of chance
I sent my piece there
On graph paper

I hear the clop of the big artillery horses trotting down the
    highroad where I stand guard
A greatcoat pencil grey like the sky shrouds me up to my ears

        Far
        Stars
        Pale
        Trail
        Of
        Faint
        Light
        From the
        Smile
Of the moon that watches me write

Ombre

Vous voilà de nouveau près de moi
Souvenirs de mes compagnons morts à la guerre
L'olive du temps
Souvenirs qui n'en faites plus qu'un
Comme cent fourrures ne font qu'un manteau
Comme ces milliers de blessures ne font qu'un article de journal
Apparence impalpable et sombre qui avez pris
La forme changeante de mon ombre
Un Indien à l'affût pendant l'éternité
Ombre vous rampez près de moi
Mais vous ne m'entendez plus
Vous ne connaîtrez plus les poèmes divins que je chante
Tandis que moi je vous entends je vous vois encore
Destinées
Ombre multiple que le soleil vous garde
Vous qui m'aimez assez pour ne jamais me quitter
Et qui dansez au soleil sans faire de poussière
Ombre encre du soleil
Écriture de ma lumière
Caisson de regrets
Un dieu qui s'humilie

Shadow

Here you are at my side again
Memories of my companions dead at war
Olive of time
Memories now all sewn into one
As a hundred furs make only one coat
As the thousands of wounds make only one newspaper article
Impalpable and sombre apparition grown
To the shifting shape of my shadow
An Indian on the lookout for all eternity
Shadow you crawl along beside me
But you no longer hear me
Nor will you know the divine poems I sing
While I hear you I see you still
Destinies
Multiple shadow may the sun watch over you
You who love me so you never will go away
Who dance in the sun without kicking up dust
Ink shadow of the sun
Script of my light
Caissons of regrets
A god who humbles himself

Reconnaissance

A Mademoiselle P . . .

Un seul bouleau crépusculaire
Pâlit au seuil de l'horizon
Où fuit la mesure angulaire
Du cœur à l'âme et la raison

Le galop bleu des souvenances

Traverse les lilas des yeux

Et les canons des indolences

Tirent mes songes vers
        les
          cieux

Reconnaissance

for Mademoiselle P . . .

A single twilit birch tree
Dims on the horizon
Vanishing point of the three
Lines of heart soul and reason

The blue hooves of memory

Bisect the lilacs of the eyes

And the cannons of indolence

Shoot my dreams toward
                    the
                         skies

Guerre

Rameau central de combat
    Contact par l'écoute
On tire dans la direction « des bruits entendus »
Les jeunes de la classe 1915
Et ces fils de fer électrisés
Ne pleurez donc pas sur les horreurs de la guerre
Avant elle nous n'avions que la surface
De la terre et des mers
Après elle nous aurons les abîmes
Le sous-sol et l'espace aviatique
Maîtres du timon
Après après
Nous prendrons toutes les joies
Des vainqueurs qui se délassent
Femmes Jeux Usines Commerce
Industrie Agriculture Métal
Feu Cristal Vitesse
Voix Regard Tact à part
Et ensemble dans le tact venu de loin
De plus loin encore
De l'Au-delà de cette terre

War

Central combat division over
    Roger loud and clear
We're firing in the direction of those 'noises' you heard
The boys of the class of '15
And these electrified wires
So do not weep over the horrors of war
Before we had only the surface
Of the earth and the sea
Afterwards we'll have the abysses
What's under the ground and skies full of airplanes
Masters at the helm
Afterwards afterwards
We'll have all the joys
Of a warrior's repose
Women Gambling Factories Commerce
Industry Agriculture Metal
Fire Crystal Speed
Voice Gaze Touch aside
And together in the touch come from afar
And from even farther
From The Beyond this earth

14 Juin 1915

On ne peut rien dire
Rien de ce qui se passe
Mais on change de Secteur
Ah! voyageur égaré
Pas de lettres
Mais l'espoir
Mais un journal
Le glaive antique de la Marseillaise de Rude
S'est changé en constellation
Il combat pour nous au ciel
Mais cela signifie surtout
Qu'il faut être de ce temps
Pas de glaive antique
Pas de Glaive
Mais l'Espoir

14 June 1915

Mum's the word
About what's happening
But we're changing Sector
Oh! Traveller you've lost your way
No letters
But hope
But a newspaper
The ancient glaive of Rude's Marseillaise
Has turned into a constellation
It fights for us up in the sky
But what this means above all
Is that you need to be of your time
No ancient glaive
No Glaive
Save Hope

Les Soupirs Du Servant De Dakar

C'est dans la cagnat en rondins voilés d'osier
Auprès des canons gris tournés vers le nord
   Que je songe au village africain
Où l'on dansait où l'on chantait où l'on faisait l'amour
     Et de longs discours
      Nobles et joyeux

   Je revois mon père qui se battit
   Contre les Achantis
   Au service des Anglais
    Je revois ma sœur au rire en folie
    Aux seins durs comme des obus
      Et je revois
   Ma mère la sorcière qui seule du village
     Méprisait le sel
    Piler le millet dans un mortier
Je me souviens du si délicat si inquiétant
Fétiche dans l'arbre
Et du double fétiche de la fécondité
Plus tard une tête coupée
Au bord d'un marécage
O pâleur de mon ennemi
C'était une tête d'argent
   Et dans le marais
C'était la lune qui luisait
C'était donc une tête d'argent
Là-haut c'était la lune qui dansait
C'était donc une tête d'argent
Et moi dans l'antre j'étais invisible
C'était donc une tête de nègre dans la nuit profonde
   Similitudes Pâleurs

The Sighs of the Dakar Gunner

In the dugout of logs behind a screen of willows
Next to grey cannons pointed north
    I am dreaming of the African village
Where we danced where we sang where we made love
        And long speeches
          Noble and joyous

      Again I see my father who fought
For the English
Against the Ashantis
    Again I see my sister laughing like crazy
    Her breasts hard as the shells of bombs
        And again I see
My mother the priestess who alone in the village
      Scorned salt
    Grinding millet in a mortar
I remember the very delicate and very disturbing
Fetish in the tree
And the twin fertility doll
Later a severed head
On the edge of a swamp
Oh paleness of my enemy
It was a silver head
    And in the marsh
It was the moon gleaming
It was a silver head then
Up above it was the moon dancing
It was a silver head then
And me in my cavern I was invisible
It was a negro head in the depths of night then
      Resemblances Pallors

Et ma sœur
Suivit plus tard un tirailleur
    Mort à Arras

Si je voulais savoir mon âge
    Il faudrait le demander à l'évêque
    Si doux si doux avec ma mère
    De beurre de beurre avec ma sœur
    C'était dans une petite cabane
Moins sauvage que notre cagnat de canonniers-servants
    J'ai connu l'affût au bord des marécages
    Où la girafe boit les jambes écartées
J'ai connu l'horreur de l'ennemi qui dévaste
        Le Village
        Viole les femmes
        Emmène les filles
Et les garçons dont la croupe dure sursaute
J'ai porté l'administrateur des semaines
        De village en village
        En chantonnant
    Et je fus domestique à Paris
            Je ne sais pas mon âge
            Mais au recrutement
            On m'a donné vingt ans
    Je suis soldat français on m'a blanchi du coup
    Secteur 59 je ne peux pas dire où
Pourquoi donc être blanc est-ce mieux qu'être noir
    Pourquoi ne pas danser et discourir
        Manger et puis dormir
    Et nous tirons sur les ravitaillements boches
    Ou sur les fils de fer devant les bobosses
    Sous la tempête métallique
        Je me souviens d'un lac affreux
    Et de couples enchaînés par un atroce amour

And my sister
Later went off with an infantryman
Who died at Arras

If I wanted to know my age
I'd have to ask the bishop
So gentle so gentle with my mother
Butter butter with my sister
It was in a little hut
Not so savage as our gunners' dugout
I know all about waiting and watching on the edges of
swamps
Where giraffes drink with spread legs
I've known the horror of the enemy who lays waste
To the Village
Rapes the women
Takes away the girls
And the boys whose hard rumps jerk
For weeks I took the administrator
From village to village
Humming a song
And I was a houseboy in Paris
I don't know my age
But when they signed me up
Twenty's the age they wrote down
I am a French soldier you might say I've been whitened
Sector 59 I can't say where or
What makes being white better than being black
Why not dance and make speeches
Eat and then sleep
And we shoot at the Boche supply lines
Or at the barbed wire in front of the doughboys
In this blizzard of metal
I remember a horrible lake
And couples chained together by an atrocious love

Une nuit folle
Une nuit de sorcellerie
Comme cette nuit-ci
Où tant d'affreux regards
Éclatent dans le ciel splendide

A crazy night
A night of witchcraft
Like tonight
Where so many horrible gazes
Explode in the resplendent sky

La Nuit d'Avril 1915

A L. de C.-C.

Le ciel est étoilé par les obus des Boches
La forêt merveilleuse où je vis donne un bal
La mitrailleuse joue un air à triples-croches
Mais avez-vous le mot
                                    Eh! oui le mot fatal
Aux créneaux Aux créneaux Laissez là les pioches

Comme un astre éperdu qui cherche ses saisons
Cœur obus éclaté tu sifflais ta romance
Et tes mille soleils ont vidé les caissons
Que les dieux de mes yeux remplissent en silence

Nous vous aimons ô vie et nous vous agaçons

Les obus miaulaient un amour à mourir
Un amour qui se meurt est plus doux que les autres
Ton souffle nage au fleuve où le sang va tarir
Les obus miaulaient
                                    Entends chanter les nôtres
Pourpre amour salué par ceux qui vont périr

Le printemps tout mouillé la veilleuse l'attaque
Il pleut mon âme il pleut mais il pleut des yeux morts

Ulysse que de jours pour rentrer dans Ithaque
Couche-toi sur la paille et songe un beau remords
Qui pur effet de l'art soit aphrodisiaque

Mais
        orgues
                aux fétus de la paille où tu dors
L'hymne de l'avenir est paradisiaque

54

The Night of April 1915

to L. de C.-C.

The sky is starred with the Boche shells
Enchanted forest I live in you're having a ball
The machine gun tootles double quick
But did you get the word
                              Oh! the word that's fatal
To the battlements To the battlements Drop your picks

Bewildered as a star in search of its seasons
Heart burst shell you whistled your romance
And your thousand suns emptied the caissons
Which the gods of my eyes refill in silence

We love you oh life and we exasperate you

The shells caterwauled a love to die for
A love that is dying is sweetest of all
Your breath swims the river where blood will run dry
The shells caterwauled
                              Listen we sing and we fall
A purple love those who go to die hail

Spring all wet the nightwatch the attack
It's raining my soul it's raining but it's raining dead eyes

Ulysses Ithaca how many days to go back
Bed down in the straw and dream a fine remorse
Remorse so artful it will be aphrodisiac

But
      organs
                for the wisps of straw that you sleep on
The hymn of the future is paradisiac

La Grâce Exilée

Va-t'en va-t'en mon arc-en-ciel
Allez-vous-en couleurs charmantes
Cet exil t'est essentiel
Infante aux écharpes changeantes

Et l'arc-en-ciel est exilé
Puisqu'on exile qui l'irise
Mais un drapeau s'est envolé
Prendre ta place au vent de bise

★

Les Feux Du Bivouac

Les feux mouvants du bivouac
Éclairent des formes de rêve
Et le songe dans l'entrelacs
Des branches lentement s'élève

Voici les dédains du regret
Tout écorché comme une fraise
Le souvenir et le secret
Dont il ne reste que la braise

★

Grace Exiled

Off you go off you go my rainbow
Off you go charming colours
Exile is what you need now
Infanta with your changing scarves

And the rainbow is exiled
Since we exile what iridesces
But look! a flag is unfurled
To take your place in the breeze

*

Bivouac Fires

The bivouac fires flickering
Illuminate the forms of dream
And in the interlacing
Branches reveries gleam

Here are the disdains of regret
Galling as a strawberry
The memory and the secret
Whose embers only remain

*

Tourbillon de Mouches

Un cavalier va dans la plaine
La jeune fille pense à lui
Et cette flotte à Mytilène
Le fil de fer est là qui luit

Comme ils cueillaient la rose ardente
Leurs yeux tout à coup ont fleuri
Mais quel soleil la bouche errante
A qui la bouche avait souri

★

L'Adieu du Cavalier

Ah Dieu! que la guerre est jolie
Avec ses chants ses longs loisirs
Cette bague je l'ai polie
Le vent se mêle à vos soupirs

Adieu! voici le boute-selle
Il disparut dans un tournant
Et mourut là-bas tandis qu'elle
Riait au destin surprenant

Swarm of Flies

A horseman rides across the plain
The girl thinks of her lover
And of that fleet at Mytilene
There's that shiny strand of wire

When they plucked the ardent rose
Their eyes burst into bloom
But what a sun the errant mouth
At which his mouth did smile

*

The Horseman's Farewell

Lord! How pretty war is
With its songs its free time
See this ring I have polished
The wind grasps at your sighs

Farewell! The trumpet sounds for me
He disappeared round a bend
And died up there while she
Laughed at what fate can send

Le Palais du Tonnerre

Par l'issue ouverte sur le boyau dans la craie
Eu regardant la paroi adverse qui semble en nougat
On voit à gauche et à droite fuir l'humide couloir désert
Où meurt étendue une pelle à la face effrayante à deux yeux
    réglementaires qui servent à l'attacher sous les caissons
Un rat y recule en hâte tandis que j'avance en hâte
Et le boyau s'en va couronné de craie semé de branches
Comme un fantôme creux qui met du vide où il passe blanchâtre
Et là-haut le toit est bleu et couvre bien le regard fermé par
    quelques lignes droites
Mais en deçà de l'issue c'est le palais bien nouveau et qui paraît
    ancien
Le plafond est fait de traverses de chemin de fer
Entre lesquelles il y a des morceaux de craie et des touffes
    d'aiguilles de sapin
Et de temps en temps des débris de craie tombent comme des
    morceaux de vieillesse
A côté de l'issue que ferme un tissu lâche d'une espèce qui sert
    généralement aux emballages
Il y a un trou qui tient lieu d'âtre et ce qui y brûle est un feu
    semblable à l'âme
Tant il tourbillonne et tant il est inséparable de ce qu'il dévore et
    fugitif
Les fils de fer se tendent partout servant de sommier supportant
    des planches
Ils forment aussi des crochets et l'on y suspend mille choses
Comme on fait à la mémoire
Des musettes bleues des casques bleus des cravates bleues des
    vareuses bleues
Morceaux du ciel tissus des souvenirs les plus purs
Et il flotte parfois en l'air, de vagues nuages de craie

The Thunder's Palace

Looking through the opening to the trench carved out of chalk
Towards the far wall that looks as if it were made of nougat
One can see to left and right dank deserted passageways fleeing
And a shovel dying flat on its back with its frightful face and the
    two eyes used to fix it to the caissons
A rat backs off as quickly as I advance
And the trench goes on and on vaulted with chalk strewn with
    branches
Like a hollow ghost leaving behind itself a ghastly emptiness
And overhead the roof is blue and stretches well over the view
    barred by a few straight lines
But on this side of the opening there's a brand-new palace that
    looks old
The roof is made of railway ties
Between them are lumps of chalk and clumps of fir needles
And now and then a piece of chalk breaks off and drops like bits
    of old age
Next to the opening closed by a flap of the kind of fabric used for
    packing
Is a hole that serves as a hearth and what is burning there is a fire
    that resembles the soul
Because of how it swirls up and how fleeting and inseparable it is
    from whatever it devours
Everywhere wires are stretched to support planks
And also bent to make hooks and we hang thousands of things
    on them
As one does with memory
Blue haversacks blue helmets blue ties blue uniform jackets
Pieces of sky fabric of the purest memories
And sometimes vague clouds of chalk hang in the air

Sur la planche brillent des fusées détonateurs joyaux dorés à tête
    émaillée
Noirs blancs rouges
Funambules qui attendent leur tour de passer sur les trajectoires
Et font un ornement mince et élégant à cette demeure
    souterraine
Ornée de six lits placés en fer à cheval
Six lits couverts de riches manteaux bleus

Sur le palais il y a un haut tumulus de craie
Et des plaques de tôle ondulée
Fleuve figé de ce domaine idéal
Mais privé d'eau car ici il ne roule que le feu jailli de la mélinite
Le parc aux fleurs de fulminate jaillit des trous penchés
Tas de cloches aux doux sons des douilles rutilantes
Sapins élégants et petits comme en un paysage japonais
Le palais s'éclaire parfois d'une bougie à la flamme aussi petite
    qu'une souris
O palais minuscule comme si on te regardait par le gros bout
    d'une lunette
Petit palais où tout s'assourdit
Petit palais où tout est neuf rien rien d'ancien
Et où tout est précieux où tout le monde est vêtu comme un roi
Une selle est dans un coin à cheval sur une caisse
Un journal du jour traîne par terre
Et cependant tout paraît vieux dans cette neuve demeure
Si bien qu'on comprend que l'amour de l'antique
Le goût de l'anticaille
Soit venu aux hommes dès le temps des cavernes
Tout y était si précieux et si neuf
Tout y est si précieux et si neuf
Qu'une chose plus ancienne ou qui a déjà servi y apparaît

On the plank flares detonators gilded jewels with enamelled
    heads shine
Black white red
Funambulists waiting their turn to shoot through the air
Slender elegant they embellish this underground mansion
Adorned with six beds that make a horseshoe shape
Six beds covered with rich blue cloaks

On top of the palace is a high chalk tumulus
And sheets of corrugated metal
Congealed river of this ideal domain
Though lacking water for here only fire springs from the
    melinite
The garden with its flowers of fulminate springs from the slant
    holes
Pile of bells that ring out with the soft sounds of the ruddy shell
    cases
Elegant fir trees small as in a Japanese landscape
The palace is sometimes lit with a candle whose flame is small as
    a mouse
O minuscule palace as if one were looking at you through the
    wrong end of a telescope
Little palace where everything is muffled
Little palace where everything is new nothing nothing old
And where everything is precious where everyone is dressed like
    a king
In a corner a saddle astride a box
One of today's papers lies on the floor
And yet everything seems old in this new dwelling
So one understands that the love of what's old
A taste for the antiquey
Must have come to men already when they lived in caves
There everything was so precious and so new
Everything is so precious and so new
That something older or which has already been used looks

                    Plus précieuse
Que ce qu'on a sous la main
Dans ce palais souterrain creusé dans la craie si blanche et si
        neuve
Et deux marches neuves
            Elles n'ont pas deux semaines
Sont si vieilles et si usées dans ce palais qui semble antique sans
        imiter l'antique
Qu'on voit que ce qu'il y a de plus simple de plus neuf est ce qui
        est
Le plus près de ce que l'on appelle la beauté antique
Et ce qui est surchargé d'ornements
A besoin de vieillir pour avoir la beauté qu'on appelle antique
Et qui est la noblesse la force l'ardeur l'âme l'usure
De ce qui est neuf et qui sert
Surtout si cela est simple simple
Aussi simple que le petit palais du tonnerre

More precious

Than what one has at hand

In this underground palace scraped out of the so white and so
new chalk

And two new steps

They aren't two weeks old

Are so old and worn in this palace which seems ancient though
without imitating the ancient

That one sees that that which is most simple and most new is
what is

Closest to what we call ancient beauty

And whatever is burdened with ornament

Needs to age to acquire the beauty one calls ancient

And which is the nobility the force the ardour the soul the luster

Of what is new and what is useful

Especially if it is plain and simple

As plain and simple as the thunder's small palace

Photographie

Ton sourire m'attire comme
Pourrait m'attirer une fleur
Photographie tu es le champignon brun
De la forêt
Qu'est sa beautè
Les blancs y sont
Un clair de lune
Dans un jardin pacifique
Plein d'eaux vives et de jardiniers endiablés
Photographie tu es la fumée de l'ardeur
Qu'est sa beauté
Et il y a en toi
Photographie
Des tons alanguis
On y entend
Une mélopée
Photographie tu es l'ombre
Du Soleil
Qu'est sa beauté

Photograph

Your smile calls to me the way
A flower might call to me
Photograph you are the brown mushroom
Of the forest
That is its beauty
The whites in it are
Moonlight
In a peaceful garden
Full of fountains playing and diabolic gardeners
Photograph you are ardour's smoke
That is its beauty
And in you
Photograph
Are languorous tones
In which one can hear
A lament
Photograph you are the shadow
Of the Sun
That is its beauty

L'Inscription Anglaise

C'est quelque chose de si ténu de si lointain
Que d'y penser on arrive à le trop matérialiser
Forme limitée par la mer bleue
Par la rumeur d'un train en marche
Par l'odeur des eucalyptus des mimosas
Et des pins maritimes

   Mais le contact et la saveur

Et cette petite voyageuse alerte inclina brusquement la tête
  sur le quai de la gare à Marseille
    Et s'en alla
    Sans savoir
Que son souvenir planerait
Sur un petit bois de la Champagne où un soldat s'efforce
Devant le feu d'un bivouac d'évoquer cette apparition
A travers la fumée d'écorce de bouleau
Qui sent l'encens minéen
Tandis que les volutes bleuâtres qui montent
D'un cigare écrivent le plus tendre des noms
Mais les nœuds de couleuvres en se dénouant
Écrivent aussi le nom émouvant
Dont chaque lettre se love en belle anglaise

Et le soldat n'ose point achever
Le jeu de mots bilingue que ne manque point de susciter
Cette calligraphie sylvestre et vernale

The English Inscription

It is a thing so tenuous so distant
That even just thinking about it can make it too solid
A form bounded by the blue sea
By the sound of the wheels of the train
By the smell of eucalyptus of mimosa
And maritime pine

    But the contact and the savour

And this alert little traveller with a quick nod on the platform
    of the Marseilles train station
        Went off
        Not knowing
That her memory would hover
Over a little wood in Champagne where a soldier
Beside the fire of a bivouac tries to conjure up that apparition
Through the birch bark's smoke
Which smells of Minean incense
While the bluish scrolls
From a cigar write the sweetest of names
But the snakes slipping their knots
Also write the touching name
Whose every letter flows in a beautiful round English hand

And the soldier doesn't dare put an end
To the bilingual wordplay that this sylvan
And vernal calligraphy cannot not conjure up

Dans L'Abri-Caverne

Je me jette vers toi et il me semble aussi que tu te jettes vers moi
Une force part de nous qui est un feu solide qui nous soude
Et puis il y a aussi une contradiction qui fait que nous ne pouvons
    nous apercevoir
En face de moi la paroi de craie s'effrite
Il y a des cassures
De longues traces d'outils traces lisses et qui semblent être faites
    dans de la stéarine
Des coins de cassures sont arrachés par le passage des types de
    ma pièce
Moi j'ai ce soir une âme qui s'est creusée qui est vide
On dirait qu'on y tombe sans cesse et sans trouver de fond
Et qu'il n'y a rien pour se raccrocher
Ce qui y tombe et qui y vit c'est une sorte d'êtres laids qui me
    font mal et qui viennent de je ne sais où
Oui je crois qu'ils viennent de la vie d'une sorte de vie qui est
    dans l'avenir dans l'avenir brut qu'on n'a pu encore cultiver
    ou élever ou humaniser
Dans ce grand vide de mon âme il manque un soleil il manque ce
    qui éclaire
C'est aujourd'hui c'est ce soir et non toujours
Heureusement que ce n'est que ce soir
Les autres jours je me rattache à toi
Les autres jours je me console de la solitude et de toutes les
    horreurs
En imaginant ta beauté
Pour l'élever au-dessus de l'univers extasié
Puis je pense que je l'imagine en vain
Je ne la connais par aucun sens
Ni même par les mots

In the Cave-Shelter

I throw myself towards you and it seems to me you also throw
    yourself towards me
A force comes from us that is a solid fire welding us together
And then there is also a kind of contradiction that makes us
    unable to see each other
Across from me the chalk wall crumbles
There are cracks
Long traces of tools smooth traces that seem to have been etched
    in stearin
In places the crack has been chipped away by hulks like me
As far as that goes tonight I have a soul that feels hollow that
    feels empty
As if one fell endlessly without ever touching the bottom
Without a single thing to hang on to
What is falling and what is alive here are some ugly beings who
    hurt me and who come from I don't know where
Yes I believe they come from life from a kind of life of the future
    from that crude future we haven't yet been able to cultivate
    or elevate or humanize
In this great void of my soul what's missing is a sun what's
    missing is what might cast some light
It's today it's this evening and not forever
Luckily it is only this evening
The other days I cling to you
The other days I console myself for the solitude and for all the
    horrors
By imagining your beauty
To hold it up above the universe in thrall
Then I think I imagine it in vain
I don't know it in any sense
Nor even by means of words

Et mon goût de la beauté est-il donc aussi vain
Existes-tu mon amour
Ou n'es-tu qu'une entité que j'ai créée sans le vouloir
Pour peupler la solitude
Es-tu une de ces déesses comme celles que les Grecs avaient
    douées pour moins s'ennuyer
Je t'adore ô ma déesse exquise même si tu n'es que dans mon
    imagination

And is my taste for beauty therefore also vain
Do you exist my love
Or are you only an entity I have created without meaning to
In order to people the solitude
Are you one of those goddesses such as the Greeks endowed
    with being in order to be less bored
Oh my exquisite goddess I adore you even if you exist only in
    my imagination

Fusée

La boucle des cheveux noirs de ta nuque est mon trésor
Ma pensée te rejoint et la tienne la croise
Tes seins sont les seuls obus que j'aime
Ton souvenir est la lanterne de repérage qui nous sert à pointer
    la nuit

En voyant la large croupe de mon cheval j'ai pensé à tes hanches

Voici les fantassins qui s'en vont à l'arrière en lisant un journal

Le chien du brancardier revient avec une pipe dans sa gueule

Un chat-huant ailes fauves yeux ternes gueule de petit chat et
    pattes de chat

Une souris verte file parmi la mousse

Le riz a brûlé dans la marmite de campement
Ça signifie qu'il faut prendre garde à bien des choses

Le mégaphone crie
Allongez le tir

Allongez le tir amour de vos batteries

Balance des batteries lourdes cymbales
Qu'agitent les chérubins fous d'amour
En l'honneur du Dieu des Armées

Un arbre dépouillé sur une butte

Flare

The curly black hair at your nape is my treasure
My thoughts are with you and they find your thoughts
Your breasts are the only bombs that I love
The memory of you is the searchlight that helps us find our
    targets at night

Seeing my horse's broad rump I thought of your hips

Here come the infantrymen going back to the rear reading their
    newspapers

The stretcher-bearer's dog comes back chewing on a pipe

A hoot-owl with tawny wings dull eyes little cat muzzle and
    paws

A green mouse scampers off through the moss

The rice burned in the camp cooking pot
This means we need to be careful about a lot of things

The megaphone blares
Lengthen the range

Lengthen the range for the love of your guns

Swing of cannons heavy cymbals
The love-crazed cherubins clash
In honour of the God of Armies

A tree stripped bare on a mound

Le bruit des tracteurs qui grimpent dans la vallée

O vieux monde du xixe siècle plein de hautes cheminées si belles
et si pures

Virilités du siècle où nous sommes
O canons

Douilles éclatantes des obus de 75
Carillonnez pieusement

Sound of tractors climbing in the valley

O old world of the XIXth century full of tall chimneys
so elegant and so pure

Virility of the present century
O cannons

75's splendidly spitting out shells
Oh holy bells

Désir

Mon désir est la région qui est devant moi
Derrière les lignes boches
Mon désir est aussi derrière moi
Après la zone des armées

Mon désir c'est la butte du Mesnil
Mon désir est là sur quoi je tire
De mon désir qui est au-delà de la zone des armées
Je n'en parle pas aujourd'hui mais j'y pense

Butte du Mesnil je t'imagine en vain
Des fils de fer des mitrailleuses des ennemis trop sûrs d'eux
Trop enfoncés sous terre déjà enterrés

Ca ta clac des coups qui meurent en s'éloignant

En y veillant tard dans la nuit
Le Decauville qui toussote
La tôle ondulée sous la pluie
Et sous la pluie ma bourguignotte

Entends la terre véhémente
Vois les lueurs avant d'entendre les coups

Et tel obus siffler de la démence
Ou le tac tac tac monotone et bref plein de dégoût

Je désire
Te serrer dans ma main Main de Massiges
Si décharnée sur la carte
Le boyau Gœthe où j'ai tiré

Desire

My desire is that region that lies straight ahead of me
Behind the Boche lines
My desire is behind me too
Behind the zone of the armies

My desire is the Butte du Mesnil
My desire is what I'm shooting at
About my desire that is beyond the military zone
I won't speak today but it's on my mind

Butte du Mesnil I picture you in vain
Barbed wire machine guns enemies swaggering
Deep underground too deep buried already

Pock-pock of shots that die off in the distance

Up late keeping watch
A Decauville coughing
Rained-on corrugated iron
My helmet my bourguignotte out in the rain

Listen to the vehement earth
See the flashes before you hear the shots

And this or that demented shell whistling
Or the sudden monotonous rat-a-tat-tat full of disgust

I want
To squeeze you in my hand Main de Massiges
So boney-looking on the map
Goethe Trench at which I've shot

J'ai tiré même sur le boyau Nietzsche
Décidément je ne respecte aucune gloire
Nuit violente et violette et sombre et pleine d'or par moments
Nuit des hommes seulement

Nuit du 24 septembre
Demain l'assaut
Nuit violente ô nuit dont l'épouvantable cri profond devenait
    plus intense de minute en minute
Nuit qui criait comme une femme qui accouche
Nuit des hommes seulement

I've even shot at Nietzsche's trench
Clearly I've no respect for anyone's glory
Dark night violent violet night at times shot through with gold
Night of men only

Night of September 24
Tomorrow the attack
Violent night O night whose dreadful throbbing cry was each
    moment growing more intense
Night which was crying like a woman in childbirth
Night of men only

Océan de Terre

A. G. de Chirico

J'ai bâti une maison au milieu de l'Océan
Ses fenêtres sont les fleuves qui s'écoulent de mes yeux
Des poulpes grouillent partout où se tiennent les murailles
Entendez battre leur triple cœur et leur bec cogner aux vitres
      Maison humide
      Maison ardente
      Saison rapide
      Saison qui chante
    Les avions pondent des œufs
    Attention on va jeter l'ancre
Attention à l'encre que l'on jette
Il serait bon que vous vinssiez du ciel
Le chèvrefeuille du ciel grimpe
Les poulpes terrestres palpitent
Et puis nous sommes tant et tant à être nos propres fossoyeurs
Pâles poulpes des vagues crayeuses ô poulpes aux becs pâles
Autour de la maison il y a cet océan que tu connais
Et qui ne se repose jamais

Ocean of Earth

for G. de Chirico

I've built myself a house in the middle of the ocean
Its windows are the rivers that flow from my eyes
Its walls are crawling with octopuses
Listen to their triple hearts beat and their beaks rap at the panes
> Dank house
> Ardent house
> Brief season
> Song season
> The airplanes are laying eggs
> Watch out we're going to drop our inkers
Watch out for the ink we splot
It would be good if you came down from the sky
Sky's honeysuckle is twisting up
Earth's octopuses pulse
Besides so many so many of us dig our own graves
Pale pulp of the chalky waves oh octopuses your pale beaks
All around my house there's this ocean as you know
That never rests

Merveille de la Guerre

Que c'est beau ces fusées qui illuminent la nuit
Elles montent sur leur propre cime et se penchent pour regarder
Ce sont des dames qui dansent avec leurs regards pour yeux bras
    et cœurs

J'ai reconnu ton sourire et ta vivacité

C'est aussi l'apothéose quotidienne de toutes mes Bérénices dont
    les chevelures sont devenues des comètes
Ces danseuses surdorées appartiennent à tous les temps et à
    toutes les races
Elles accouchent brusquement d'enfants qui n'ont que le temps
    de mourir

Comme c'est beau toutes ces fusées
Mais ce serait bien plus beau s'il y en avait plus encore
S'il y en avait des millions qui auraient un sens complet et relatif
    comme les lettres d'un livre
Pourtant c'est aussi beau que si la vie même sortait des mourants

Mais ce serait plus beau encore s'il y en avait plus encore
Cependant je les regarde comme une beauté qui s'offre et
    s'évanouit aussitôt
Il me semble assister à un grand festin éclairé a giorno
C'est un banquet que s'offre la terre
Elle a faim et ouvre de longues bouches pâles
La terre a faim et voici son festin de Balthasar cannibale

Wonder of War

How beautiful these flares are that light up the night
They climb to their own peaks and lean out to gawk
They are ladies who dance with their glances for eyes arms and
    hearts

I recognized your smile and your vivaciousness

They are also the daily apotheosis of all my Berenices whose
    ponytails turn into comets
These glittery dancers belong to all times and all races
Before you know it they give birth to children who've only time
    to die

How beautiful these flares
But it would be much more beautiful if we had even more of
    them
If there were millions whose meaning was both complete and
    relative like the letters in a book
Still it is as beautiful as if life itself issued from the dying

But it would be even more beautiful if we had many more of
    them
I look at them like some beauty who offers herself and then
    faints
I feel as if I were a guest at some great feast lit up a giorno
Earth is throwing herself a banquet
Hungry she opens long pale mouths
Earth is hungry and this is her cannibal Balthazar's feast

Qui aurait dit qu'on pût être à ce point anthropophage
Et qu'il fallût tant de feu pour rôtir le corps humain
C'est pourquoi l'air a un petit goût empyreumatique qui n'est ma
    foi pas désagréable
Mais le festin serait plus beau encore si le ciel y mangeait avec la
    terre
Il n'avale que les âmes
Ce qui est une façon de ne pas se nourrir
Et se contente de jongler avec des feux versicolores

Mais j'ai coulé dans la douceur de cette guerre avec toute ma
    compagnie au long des longs boyaux
Quelques cris de flamme annoncent sans cesse ma présence
J'ai creusé le lit où je coule en me ramifiant en mille petits fleuves
    qui vont partout
Je suis dans la tranchée de première ligne et cependant je suis
    partout ou plutôt je commence à être partout
C'est moi qui commence cette chose des siècles à venir
Ce sera plus long à réaliser que non la fable d'Icare volant

Je lègue à l'avenir l'histoire de Guillaume Apollinaire
Qui fut à la guerre et sut être partout
Dans les villes heureuses de l'arrière
Dans tout le reste de l'univers
Dans ceux qui meurent en piétinant dans le barbelé
Dans les femmes dans les canons dans les chevaux
Au zénith au nadir aux 4 points cardinaux
Et dans l'unique ardeur de cette veillée d'armes

Et ce serait sans doute bien plus beau
Si je pouvais supposer que toutes ces choses dans lesquelles je
    suis partout
Pouvaient m'occuper aussi
Mais dans ce sens il n'y a rien de fait
Car si je suis partout à cette heure il n'y a cependant que moi qui
    suis en moi

Who'd have thought we could be such cannibals
That it would take so much fire to roast the human body
That's why the air has a slight acrid taste which isn't if I may say
    disagreeable
But the feast would be even more beautiful if the heavens sat
    down with the earth
It only gobbles up souls
Which is a way of not feeding itself
All it wants to do is juggle with the flares' changing colours

But I have flowed into the sweetness of this war along the long
    trenches with my whole company
The flames' screams keep announcing my presence
I've dug the bed in which I flow branching out into thousands of
    little rivers that go everywhere
I am in the first line of trenches and yet I am everywhere or
    rather I'm beginning to be everywhere
It's me who begins this thing of the centuries to come
It will take more time to happen than the tale of Icarus flying

I leave to the future the story of Guillaume Apollinaire
Who went to war and knew how to be everywhere
In the happy cities behind the lines
In the whole rest of the universe
In those who die walking into coils of barbed wire
In the women in the cannons in the horses
At the zenith at the nadir at the 4 cardinal points
And in the particular ardour of this night's watch

And it would no doubt be much more beautiful
If I could think that all these things in which I am everywhere
Could be in me as well
But as for this everything remains to be done
For if right now I am everywhere there is however only me who
    is in me

Exercice

Vers un village de l'arrière
S'en allaient quatre bombardiers
Ils étaient couverts de poussière
Depuis la tête jusqu'aux pieds

Ils regardaient la vaste plaine
En parlant entre eux du passé
Et ne se retournaient qu'à peine
Quand un obus avait toussé

Tous quatre de la classe seize
Parlaient d'antan non d'avenir
Ainsi se prolongeait l'ascèse
Qui les exerçait à mourir

Basic Training

Four bombardiers
All covered in dust
Marched off towards a village
A village in the rear

Gazing over the vast plain
They talked about the past
Didn't turn to look
When a shell coughed

So all four class of '16
Talking of yore not the future
Signed on for more
Basic training in death

Il y a

Il y a un vaisseau qui a emporté ma bien-aimée
Il y a dans le ciel six saucisses et la nuit venant on dirait des
    asticots dont naîtraient les étoiles
Il y a un sous-marin ennemi qui en voulait à mon amour
Il y a mille petits sapins brisés par les éclats d'obus autour de moi
Il y a un fantassin qui passe aveuglé par les gaz asphyxiants
Il y a que nous avons tout haché dans les boyaux de Nietzsche de
    Gœthe et de Cologne
Il y a que je languis après une lettre qui tarde
Il y a dans mon porte-cartes plusieurs photos de mon amour
Il y a les prisonniers qui passent la mine inquiète
Il y a une batterie dont les servants s'agitent autour des pièces
Il y a le vaguemestre qui arrive au trot par le chemin de l'Arbre
    isolé
Il y a dit-on un espion qui rôde par ici invisible comme l'horizon
    dont il s'est indignement revêtu et avec quoi il se confond
Il y a dressé comme un lys le buste de mon amour
Il y a un capitaine qui attend avec anxiété les communications de
    la T. S. F. sur l'Atlantique
Il y a à minuit des soldats qui scient des planches pour les
    cercueils
Il y a des femmes qui demandent du maïs à grands cris devant un
    Christ sanglant à Mexico
Il y a le Gulf Stream qui est si tiède et si bienfaisant
Il y a un cimetière plein de croix à 5 kilomètres
Il y a des croix partout de-ci de-là
Il y a des figues de Barbarie sur ces cactus en Algérie
Il y a les longues mains souples de mon amour
Il y a un encrier que j'avais fait dans une fusée de 15 centimètres
    et qu'on n'a pas laissé partir
Il y a ma selle exposée à la pluie

There's

There's a ship that sailed away with my love
There are six sausages in the sky and at nightfall you'd think
  they were maggots giving birth to the stars
There's an enemy submarine out of sorts with my love
There are thousands of little pine trees broken by the shells that
  are bursting all around me
There's an infantryman going by blinded by gas
There's that we've diced the tripe of Nietzsche Goethe and
  Cologne
There's that I long for a letter that hasn't come
There are in my wallet several photos of my love
There are prisoners going by with anxious faces
There's a battery whose gunners bustle around the guns
There's the post orderly coming jogging along Lone Tree Road
There is they say a spy prowling round invisible as the horizon
  he's brazenly put on and into which he blends
There's my love's bust sitting tall as a lily
There's a captain who's anxiously expecting news from the
  Atlantic on the TSF
There are soldiers at midnight sawing planks for coffins
There are women screaming for corn in front of a bloody Christ
  in Mexico
There's the Gulf Stream which is so warm and so good for us
There's a cemetery full of crosses 5 kilometres away
There are crosses everywhere you look
There are Barbary figs on those cactuses in Algeria
There are my love's long graceful hands
There's an inkwell I made in a flare 15 centimetres long which
  they wouldn't send off
There's my saddle left out in the rain

Il y a les fleuves qui ne remontent pas leur cours
Il y a l'amour qui m'entraîne avec douceur
Il y avait un prisonnier boche qui portait sa mitrailleuse sur son
    dos
Il y a des hommes dans le monde qui n'ont jamais été à la guerre
Il y a des Hindous qui regardent avec étonnement les campagnes
    occidentales
Ils pensent avec mélancolie à ceux dont ils se demandent s'ils les
    reverront
Car on a poussé très loin durant cette guerre l'art de l'invisibilité

There are the rivers that don't return to their sources
There is love that bears me gently along
There was a Boche prisoner carrying his machine gun on his
    back
There are men in the world who've never been to war
There are some Hindus who look with astonishment at our
    Western countrysides
They think sadly of those they are wondering if they will ever
    see again
For the art of invisibility has made great strides in this war

Le Vigneron Champenois

Le régiment arrive
Le village est presque endormi dans la lumière parfumée
Un prêtre a le casque en tête
La bouteille champenoise est-elle ou non une artillerie
Les ceps de vigne comme l'hermine sur un écu
Bonjour soldats
Je les ai vus passer et repasser en courant
Bonjour soldats bouteilles champenoises où le sang fermente
Vous resterez quelques jours et puis remonterez en ligne
Échelonnés ainsi que sont les ceps de vigne
J'envoie mes bouteilles partout comme les obus d'une charmante
    artillerie

La nuit est blonde ô vin blond
Un vigneron chantait courbé dans sa vigne
Un vigneron sans bouche au fond de l'horizon
Un vigneron qui était lui-même la bouteille vivante
Un vigneron qui sait ce qu'est la guerre
Un vigneron champenois qui est un artilleur

C'est maintenant le soir et l'on joue à la mouche
Puis les soldats s'en iront là-haut
Où l'Artillerie débouche ses bouteilles crémantes
Allons Adieu messieurs tâchez de revenir
Mais nul ne sait ce qui peut advenir

The Grape Grower in Champagne

The regiment arrives
The village dozes off in the perfumed light
A priest has a helmet on his head
Is the champagne bottle artillery or not
The vinestock like ermine on a coat of arms
Bonjour soldiers
I saw them racing this way and that
Bonjour soldiers champagne bottles in which blood ferments
You'll stay a few days then back to the front
In your echelons like a field planted with vines
I send my bottles all over the place like the shells of a delightful
    artillery

The night is blond oh blond wine
A grape-grower was singing bent over his vines
A grape-grower without a mouth on the far horizon
A grape-grower who himself was the living bottle
A grape-grower who knows all about war
A grape-grower in Champagne who's an artilleryman

Now it's evening and they're playing poker
Then the soldiers will return to the front
Where the Artillery uncorks its foaming bottles
Well Adieu gentlemen come back if you can
But who's to say what the future has planned

Carte Postale

Je t'écris de dessous la tente
Tandis que meurt ce jour d'été
Où floraison éblouissante
Dans le ciel à peine bleuté
Une canonnade éclatante
Se fane avant d'avoir été

Postcard

I'm in my tent writing to you
As this summer day dies
And in a dazzling display of bloom
Against a sky faintly blue
A spectacular cannonade
Fades before it can rise

L'Avenir

Soulevons la paille
Regardons la neige
Écrivons des lettres
Attendons des ordres

Fumons la pipe
En songeant à l'amour
Les gabions sont là
Regardons la rose

La fontaine n'a pas tari
Pas plus que l'or de la paille ne s'est terni
Regardons l'abeille
Et ne songeons pas à l'avenir

Regardons nos mains
Qui sont la neige
La rose et l'abeille
Ainsi que l'avenir

The Future

Let's lift up the straw
Let's look at the snow
Let's write some letters
Let's wait for orders

Let's smoke a pipe
While we dream about love
There are the gabions
Let's look at the rose

The fountain hasn't gone dry
Nor the straw's gold dull
Let's look at the bee
And not think of the future

Let's look at our hands
Which are the snow
The rose and the bee
And also the future

Chevaux de Frise

Pendant le blanc et nocturne novembre
Alors que les arbres déchiquetés par l'artillerie
Vieillissaient encore sous la neige
Et semblaient à peine des chevaux de frise
Entourés de vagues de fils de fer
Mon cœur renaissait comme un arbre au printemps
Un arbre fruitier sur lequel s'épanouissent
                    Les fleurs de l'amour

Pendant le blanc et nocturne novembre
Tandis que chantaient épouvantablement les obus
Et que les fleurs mortes de la terre exhalaient
                    Leurs mortelles odeurs
Moi je décrivais tous les jours mon amour à Madeleine
La neige met de pâles fleurs sur les arbres
            Et toisonne d'hermine les chevaux de frise
                Que l'on voit partout
                    Abandonnés et sinistres
                    Chevaux muets
                Non chevaux barbes mais barbelés
                    Et je les anime tout soudain
                En troupeau de jolis chevaux pies
Qui vont vers toi comme de blanches vagues
                Sur la Méditerranée
                Et t'apportent mon amour
Roselys ô panthère ô colombes étoile bleue
                O Madeleine
Je t'aime avec délices
Si je songe à tes yeux je songe aux sources fraîches
Si je pense à ta bouche les roses m'apparaissent
Si je songe à tes seins le Paraclet descend

Chevaux-de-frise

During the white and nocturnal November
While the trees the artillery had hacked
Aged even more as the snow fell
They weren't even chevaux-de-frise
Surrounded by waves of barbed wire
My heart was being reborn like a tree in spring
A fruit tree on which love's flowers
    Are coming into bloom

During the white and nocturnal November
While the shells were horribly singing
And earth's dead flowers exhaled
   Their mortal odours
Every day I'd describe my love to Madeleine
Snow puts pale flowers on the trees
   And tufts of ermine on the chevaux-de-frise
    You see them everywhere
    Abandoned and sinister
    Mute horses
   Not Barb horses but barbed wire
    And suddenly I can bring them to life
  A pretty troop of piebald horses
Galloping towards you like white waves
    On the Mediterranean
    Bringing you my love
Roselily oh panther oh doves blue star
    Oh Madeleine
I delight in my love for you
If I think of your eyes I think of cool springs
If I think of your mouth roses appear to me
If I think of your breasts the Paraclete descends

O double colombe de ta poitrine
Et vient délier ma langue de poète
Pour te redire
Je t'aime
Ton visage est un bouquet de fleurs
Aujourd'hui je te vois non Panthère
Mais Toutefleur
Et je te respire ô ma Toutefleur
Tous les lys montent en toi comme des cantiques d'amour et
d'allégresse
Et ces chants qui s'envolent vers toi
M'emportent à ton côté
Dans ton bel Orient où les lys
Se changent en palmiers qui de leurs belles mains
Me font signe de venir
La fusée s'épanouit fleur nocturne
Quand il fait noir
Et elle retombe comme une pluie de larmes amoureuses
De larmes heureuses que la joie fait couler
Et je t'aime comme tu m'aimes
Madeleine

Oh twin doves of your breast
And comes to unknot my poet's tongue
To tell you again
I love you
Your face is a bouquet of flowers
Today I see you not Panther
But Allflower
And I breathe you in oh my Allflower
All the lilies rise up in you like canticles of joy and love
And these songs that go flying towards you
Bring me to your side
In your beautiful Orient where the lilies
Become palm trees which with their beautiful hands
Beckon to me
The flare unfolds nocturnal flower
After dark
And it falls like a rain of amorous tears
Happy tears falling for joy
And I love you as you love me
Madeleine

Chef de Section

Ma bouche aura des ardeurs de géhenne
Ma bouche te sera un enfer de douceur et de séduction
Les anges de ma bouche trôneront dans ton cœur
Les soldats de ma bouche te prendront d'assaut
Les prêtres de ma bouche encenseront ta beauté
Ton âme s'agitera comme une région pendant un tremblement
    de terre
Tes yeux seront alors chargés de tout l'amour qui s'est amassé
    dans les regards de l'humanité depuis qu'elle existe
Ma bouche sera une armée contre toi une armée pleine de
    disparates
Variée comme un enchanteur qui sait varier ses métamorphoses
L'orchestre et les chœurs de ma bouche te diront mon amour
Elle te le murmure de loin
Tandis que les yeux fixés sur la montre j'attends la minute
    prescrite pour l'assaut

Platoon Leader

My mouth will be as ardent as Gehenna's fires
For you my mouth is going to be a hell of sweetness and
    seduction
The angels of my mouth will lord it over your heart
The soldiers of my mouth will take you by storm
The priests of my mouth will sing praise to your beauty
Your soul will shake like the epicentre of an earthquake
Then your eyes will fill with all the love that has gathered in the
    gaze of humanity from its beginning
My mouth will be an army against you an army of irregulars
As varied as a magician who knows how to vary his
    metamorphoses
The orchestra and choirs of my mouth will tell you my love
They murmur it to you from afar
While with my eyes glued to my watch I await the moment
    prescribed for the attack

La Victoire

Un coq chante je rêve et les feuillards agitent
Leurs feuilles qui ressemblent à de pauvres marins

Ailés et tournoyants comme Icare le faux
Des aveugles gesticulant comme des fourmis
Se miraient sous la pluie aux reflets du trottoir

Leurs rires amassés en grappes de raisin

Ne sors plus de chez moi diamant qui parlais
Dors doucement tu es chez toi tout t'appartient
Mon lit ma lampe et mon casque troué

Regards précieux saphirs taillés aux environs de Saint-Claude
    Les jours étaient une pure émeraude

Je me souviens de toi ville des météores
Ils fleurissaient en l'air pendant ces nuits où rien ne dort
Jardins de la lumière où j'ai cueilli des bouquets

Tu dois en avoir assez de faire peur à ce ciel
            Qu'il garde son hoquet

On imagine difficilement
A quel point le succès rend les gens stupides et tranquilles

    A l'institut des jeunes aveugles on a demandé
    N'avez-vous point de jeune aveugle ailé

O bouches l'homme est à la recherche d'un nouveau langage
Auquel le grammairien d'aucune langue n'aura rien à dire

Victory

A cock crows I dream and branches flutter
Their leaves that look like poor sailor boys

With wings and spinning like Icarus the false
Some blind people gesticulating like ants
Were mirrored in the rain in the gleaming sidewalks

Their laughs came in bunches like clusters of grapes

Stay here at home with me diamond of speech
Sweetly sleep make yourself at home here everything is yours
My bed my lamp and my punctured helmet

Precious gazes sapphires cut in the vicinity of Saint-Claude
  The days were pure emerald

I remember you city of meteors
At night when nothing sleeps they would blossom in the air
The gardens of light where I picked myself a few bouquets

You must be fed up scaring the sky
          Let it keep its hiccoughs

You can't imagine
How cow-like success makes people

  At the School for the Blind someone asked
  Haven't you any blind scholars with wings

Oh mouths men are seeking a new language
Which no grammarian of any language will find fault with

Et ces vieilles langues sont tellement près de mourir
Que c'est vraiment par habitude et manque d'audace
Qu'on les fait encore servir à la poésie

Mais elles sont comme des malades sans volonté
Ma foi les gens s'habitueraient vite au mutisme
La mimique suffit bien au cinéma

      Mais entêtons-nous à parler
      Remuons la langue
      Lançons des postillons
On veut de nouveaux sons de nouveaux sons de nouveaux sons
On veut des consonnes sans voyelles
Des consonnes qui pètent sourdement
      Imitez le son de la toupie
Laissez pétiller un son nasal et continu
Faites claquer votre langue
Servez-vous du bruit sourd de celui qui mange sans civilité
Le raclement aspiré du crachement ferait aussi une belle
    consonne

Les divers pets labiaux rendraient aussi vos discours claironnants
Habituez-vous à roter à volonté
Et quelle lettre grave comme un son de cloche
      A travers nos mémoires
Nous n'aimons pas assez la joie
De voir les belles choses neuves
O mon amie hâte-toi
Crains qu'un jour un train ne t'émeuve
      Plus
Regarde-le plus vite pour toi
Ces chemins de fer qui circulent
Sortiront bientôt de la vie
Ils seront beaux et ridicules
Deux lampes brûlent devant moi

And these old languages are so close to death
Truly it's out of habit and for lack of daring
That we still use them for poetry

But they are like sick people without volition
I swear people would soon get used to silence
Miming works just fine in the movies

      But let's keep trying to talk
      Flap our tongues
      Let's splutter and spit
Let's have new sounds new sounds new sounds
Let's have consonants without vowels
Consonants that softly fart
      Imitate the whirr of tops spinning
Let some long nasal sound bubble up
Clack your tongue
Make slurps like some lout eating
The sound of hawking before spitting would also be a great
    consonant

Various labial farts would make your words ring out
Belch as much as you like
Learn which letter cuts like the sound of a bell
      Through our memories
We don't yet appreciate the joy
Of seeing the beautiful new things
Oh my friend hurry up
Fear the day a train no longer
Sends shivers down your spine
Hurry up look at it it's for you
These trains that roll down their tracks
Will soon vanish from our lives
They'll be beautiful and ridiculous
Two lamps glow in front of me

Comme deux femmes qui rient
Je courbe tristement la tête
Devant l'ardente moquerie
Ce rire se répand
Partout
Parlez avec les mains faites claquer vos doigts
Tapez-vous sur la joue comme sur un tambour
                    O paroles
            Elles suivent dans la myrtaie
            L'Éros et l'Antéros en larmes
Je suis le ciel de la cité

                    Écoutez la mer

La mer gémir au loin et crier toute seule
            Ma voix fidèle comme l'ombre
            Veut être enfin l'ombre de la vie
Veut être ô mer vivante infidèle comme toi

La mer qui a trahi des matelots sans nombre
Engloutit mes grands cris comme des dieux noyés
Et la mer au soleil ne supporte que l'ombre
Que jettent des oiseaux les ailes éployées

La parole est soudaine et c'est un Dieu qui tremble
Avance et soutiens-moi je regrette les mains
De ceux qui les tendaient et m'adoraient ensemble
Quelle oasis de bras m'accueillera demain
Connais-tu cette joie de voir des choses neuves

O voix je parle le langage de la mer
Et dans le port la nuit les dernières tavernes
Moi qui suis plus têtu que non l'hydre de Lerne

Like two women who are laughing
Sadly I hang my head
At their ardent mockery
This laughter spreads
Everywhere
Talk with your hands snap your fingers
Slap your cheek like a drum
                Oh words
        In the myrtle grove they follow
        Eros and Anteros weeping
I am the sky of the city

        Listen to the sea

The sea moaning in the offing and crying all alone
        My voice faithful as a shadow
        Wants to be life's shadow at last
Wants to be as faithless as you are oh living sea

The sea that has betrayed countless sailors
Swallows my great cries like drowned gods
And in the sun the sea has only the shadow
Cast by birds with their wings outspread

The word is sudden and it is a God that trembles
Come close and hold me I miss the hands
Held out to me by all those who adored me
What an oasis of arms tomorrow to greet me
Have you experienced the joy of seeing new things

Oh voice I speak the language of the sea
And in the harbour the night of the last taverns
I who am more stubborn than the Hydra of Lerna

La rue où nagent mes deux mains
Aux doigts subtils fouillant la ville
S'en va mais qui sait si demain
La rue devenait immobile
Qui sait où serait mon chemin
Songe que les chemins de fer
Seront démodés et abandonnés dans peu de temps
Regarde

La Victoire avant tout sera
De bien voir au loin
De tout voir
De près
Et que tout ait un nom nouveau

The street where my two hands swim
Their subtle fingers probing the city
Goes away but who knows if tomorrow
The street stopped moving
Who knows where the road would take me
Just think that railroads will
Soon be out of date and abandoned
Look

Victory will be above all
To see the future clearly
To see everything
Close up
And that everything have a new name

La Jolie Rousse

Me voici devant tous un homme plein de sens
Connaissant la vie et de la mort ce qu'un vivant peut connaître
Ayant éprouvé les douleurs et les joies de l'amour
Ayant su quelquefois imposer ses idées
Connaissant plusieurs langages
Ayant pas mal voyagé
Ayant vu la guerre dans l'Artillerie et l'Infanterie
Blessé à la tête trépané sous le chloroforme
Ayant perdu ses meilleurs amis dans l'effroyable lutte
Je sais d'ancien et de nouveau autant qu'un homme seul pourrait
    des deux savoir
Et sans m'inquiéter aujourd'hui de cette guerre
Entre nous et pour nous mes amis
Je juge cette longue querelle de la tradition et de l'invention
                De l'Ordre et de l'Aventure

Vous dont la bouche est faite à l'image de celle de Dieu
Bouche qui est l'ordre même
Soyez indulgents quand vous nous comparez
A ceux qui furent la perfection de l'ordre
Nous qui quêtons partout l'aventure

Nous ne sommes pas vos ennemis
Nous voulons vous donner de vastes et d'étranges domaines
Où le mystère en fleurs s'offre à qui veut le cueillir
Il y a là des feux nouveaux des couleurs jamais vues
Mille phantasmes impondérables
Auxquels il faut donner de la réalité

Nous voulons explorer la bonté contrée énorme où tout se tait

The Pretty Redhead

I stand before you all a sensible man
Conversant with life and whatever the living can know of death
Having experienced the pain and joy of love
Having now and then convinced others of his opinions
Knowing several languages
Having travelled a good deal
Having seen war in the Artillery and the Infantry
Shot in the head chloroformed and trepanned
Having lost his best friends in the terrible fight
I know as much about the ancient and the modern as any man
And setting aside for today my concern about this war
Between us and for us my friends
I'm going to judge this long quarrel concerning tradition and
  invention
          Concerning Order and Adventure

You whose mouth is made in God's image
Mouth which is itself order
We beg your indulgence when you compare us
To those who were paragons of order
We who everywhere set out in quest of adventure

We are not your enemies
We want to offer you some vast and strange domains
Where mystery holds out its flower to whoever would pick it
There are new fires colours never before seen
A thousand imponderable fantasies
To be made real

We want to explore this bounty a huge country where
  everything is silent

Il y a aussi le temps qu'on peut chasser ou faire revenir
Pitié pour nous qui combattons toujours aux frontières
De l'illimité et de l'avenir
Pitié pour nos erreurs pitié pour nos péchés

Voici que vient l'été la saison violente
Et ma jeunesse est morte ainsi que le printemps
O Soleil c'est le temps de la Raison ardente
                Et j'attends
Pour la suivre toujours la forme noble et douce
Qu'elle prend afin que je l'aime seulement
Elle vient et m'attire ainsi qu'un fer l'aimant
          Elle a l'aspect charmant
          D'une adorable rousse

Ses cheveux sont d'or on dirait
Un bel éclair qui durerait
Ou ces flammes qui se pavanent
Dans les roses-thé qui se fanent

Mais riez riez de moi
Hommes de partout surtout gens d'ici
Car il y a tant de choses que je n'ose vous dire
Tant de choses que vous ne me laisseriez pas dire
Ayez pitié de moi

There's time as well that we can get rid of or bring back
Have pity on us who are forever skirmishing on the borders
Of the boundless and the future
Pity for our errors pity for our sins

Summer is coming the violent season
And my youth is dead as is spring
Oh Sun it is time for ardent Reason
              And before I follow her
Forever I'm waiting for the noble and sweet form
She'll put on so that I love her and her only
She comes and attracts me as a magnet attracts iron
        She comes in the shape
        Of an adorable redhead

Her hair is made of gold one might say
A gorgeous flash of lightning that lasts
Or flames dancing
In tea roses fading

Go ahead laugh at me
Men from all over especially from right here
For there are so many things I don't dare say
So many things you wouldn't allow me to say
Have pity on me

Translator's Notes

I am indebted to the Pléiade edition of *Oeuvres Poétiques* (Gallimard, 1965); to the *Album Apollinaire* (Gallimard,1971); to *Lettres à Madeleine* (Gallimard, 2005); and to previous translations of Apollinaire's poems, especially Robert Shattuck's *Selected Writings of Guillaume Apollinaire* (New Directions, 1971), Anne Hyde Greet's *Calligrammes: Poems of Peace and War* (University of California, 1980), for their fine notes; Olivier Bernard's *Selected Poems* (Anvil, 1965) and Samuel Beckett's 'Zone' (Dolmen, 1972). All errors of omission and commission are, of course, my responsibility.

from *Alcools*

'Zone'

Apollinaire placed his poem 'Zone' first in his collection *Alcools* (1913), although it was the last poem he wrote before the book's publication: its disjunctive narrative structure referring to his childhood, schooldays in Monaco, Cannes and Nice, his travels and his love affairs, its ambiguous pronoun use, variable-length 'prosy' line and irregular rhymes break with the Symbolist aesthetic of *Alcools* and announce the innovative poems of *Calligrammes* (1918). A poetic manifesto, 'Zone' calls for a radical new language and style in keeping with prewar social changes and links Apollinaire to the Italian Futurists' celebration of modernity. Apollinaire eliminated punctuation in *Alcools* and *Calligrammes*, calling it 'unnecessary . . . rhythm and line length are the real punctuation'. 'Zone' is mostly, though not entirely, rhymed in couplets.

'Zone': Gabrielle Buffet-Picabia tells of visiting a village in the Jura, on the edge of an area known as 'the Zone', in October 1912 with Apollinaire, Francis Picabia and Marcel Duchamp. Apollinaire recited from his poem – as yet unnamed, he said. Then suddenly he added: 'I shall call it "Zone".' (From *Samuel Beckett: Collected Poems*, ed. Seán Lawlor and John Pilling; Faber, 2012.)

'Zone' is a word with a long history in French; it may have appealed to Apollinaire for its wide use and tonal range. 'La Zone militaire' or simply 'la zone' was the term for the area immediately outside Paris's fortifications, often filled with illegal dwellings. A 'zonard,' implying seediness, is an inhabitant of the or a zone; and the verb 'zoner' is slang for leading a precarious, marginal life.

And you whom the windows are watching . . . This morning I saw a pretty street: Apollinaire sometimes refers to himself as 'I', sometimes as 'you'. (Rimbaud, in 1871, is often seen as the initiator of this deconstruction of the self, proclaiming, *'Je est un autre.'*)

René Dalize: Apollinaire's childhood friend, René Dupuy ('Dalize' was a pseudonym). He was killed on 7 May 1917 during the attack on Cogne-le-Vent.

Love-sickness makes a lump in your throat: probably a reference to Marie Laurencin, part of the group of painters around Picasso, Derain and Braque. Laurencin married the German painter Otto de Waetjen in 1914.

an inn near Prague: Apollinaire travelled in Germany, Bohemia and Austria in 1901–2 as French tutor to the Countess of Milhau's daughter.

they throw you in jail: in 1911 Apollinaire went to jail in connection with the theft of artworks from the Louvre. Though he was quickly released, the experience was traumatic.

Rue des Rosiers: the Jewish quarter, in the Marais.

your fetishes from Polynesia or Guinea: these recall the Cubist painters' interest in Aboriginal art.

Auteil: Apollinaire lived on the Rue Gros, in Auteuil on the Right Bank from October 1909 until January 1913, when he moved to 202 Boulevard Saint-Germain on the Left Bank.

Sun neck cut: 'Single stalkless flower' Philip Larkin was to write in his poem 'Solar' (*High Windows*, 1974).

from *Calligrammes*

The name 'Calligrammes' comes from the 'concrete' poems, in which the printed letters are arranged to produce a visual effect (for instance, lines of print falling like slanting columns of rain in a poem [not included] called 'It's Raining'). Published in 1918, the poems of *Calligrammes* are arranged in six sections. The poems of the first section, predate the war; they catalogue the sights and sounds of Paris, its artistic milieux and street scenes, and were to have been collected under the title *Me Too, I'm a Painter*. The other five sections of *Calligrammes* – 'Banners', *Case d'Armons* (printed at the battlefront as a pamphlet), 'Gunfire Gleams', 'Shells the Colour of the Moon' and 'The Starry Head' – are war poems, ending with 'The Pretty Redhead', a postwar love poem and poetic manifesto.

'Windows'

'Windows' was written for the catalogue of the 1913 Robert Delaunay exhibit in Germany. Some of Apollinaire's friends claim it was written in a café as a collaborative effort; Sonia and Robert Delaunay said the poem was composed in their studio and refers to the studio window, curtain, sea urchins and an old pair of yellow shoes. Perhaps, drafted in a café, the poem was completed in the studio. 'I did my best to simplify poetic syntax and sometimes I succeeded, notably in one poem, "Windows",' Apollinaire wrote to his fiancée Madeleine in 1915; and later, 'I really, really like "Windows".' The poem also shows Apollinaire's fascination with trains and airplanes and travel in general: in 1913 his brother Albert had emigrated to Mexico.

'Monday Rue Christine'

Like 'Windows', 'Monday Rue Christine' (in Paris's 6th arrondissement near the Seine) is a 'conversation' poem: snippets of conversation are collaged together. Jacques Dyssord recalled its composition: 'We spent the evening in a little café rue Christine . . . I was leaving for Tunis the next day . . . we were the only customers. A waitress with fiery hair and freckles served us drinks . . . Apollinaire scribbled one of his best poems there on the edge of the table, based on our conversation.' The last line of this poem in French is ambiguous: 'la quinte major' is a major fifth in music, a straight in poker, as well as an old expression for slapping someone's face.

That seems to add up: in French *Ça a l'air de rimer. Rimer* can mean rhyme (there are no rhymes); it is also used in colloquialisms, such as *A quoi ça rime?*, 'What's the meaning of that?', and *Ça ne rime à rien*, 'That doesn't add up; that's completely off the wall.'

'A Ghost of Clouds'

This narrative poem, which may have started out as a short story, is set on Bastille Day, the French national holiday, 14 July.

saltimbancos: street performers, acrobats, clowns, recalling such figures in Picasso's Blue and Rose Period (1901–6) paintings, or, half a century earlier, Baudelaire's 'The Old Saltimbanco' (*Le Spleen de Paris*), in which Baudelaire, as sardonic as Apollinaire is tender, writes of the weight-lifters: 'The Hercules, proud of their enormous members, without a brow and without a brain, like orang-outangs, relax majestically in singlets washed the previous evening for the occasion.'

Recall also Baudelaire's 1864 prose poem 'Les Vocations' (*Le Spleen de Paris*), in which a boy describes his fascination with a trio of itinerant musicians, possibly gypsies: 'Their big dark eyes lit up when they were making music; a music so surprising it made you want to dance, or weep, or both at once, and you'd go mad if you listened too long. One, drawing his bow across his violin, seemed to recount a chagrin, and the other, making his little hammer hop over the strings of a small piano hung from a strap around his neck, seemed to be making fun of his neighbour's sad song, while the third banged his cymbals from time to time with extraordinary violence.'

Boulevard Saint Germain: in January 1913 Apollinaire moved to a tiny attic apartment at 202 boulevard Saint-Germain, not far from the Place Saint Germain des Près, in the 6th arrondissement. He lived here until his death in 1918.

and on a little square . . . Danton's statue: Carrefour de l'Odéon. The house Danton lived in at the time of the Revolution was once here. The statue, with its square, metro stop, cafés and cinemas, is still a popular meeting place.

Longwy: a town in north-eastern France.

that rose-violet colour: as, perhaps, in Picasso's Blue and Rose Period paintings of acrobats and clowns.

122

'The Little Auto'

Apollinaire left Deauville to drive back to Paris on 31 July 1914. The August 14 date has puzzled critics, who wonder if he changed the date to echo a popular song. Apollinaire volunteered on 10 August, was mobilized on 5 December and immediately left for Nîmes, in the south of France, to join the 38th regiment of field artillery. André Rouveyre was a writer (and disciple of Mallarmé) and graphic artist. He died in 1962.

Furious giants were rising: this stanza and the following one depend in part for their effect upon a repetitive use of the imperfect tense ('se dressaient', etc.), which can be rendered by the continuous ('were rising up') or the simple past tense ('rose up') in English. I have chosen to use almost entirely the heavier-sounding continuous (-ing) form, to emphasize, as I think Apollinaire has emphasized, the inexorability of events.

Francorchamps . . . Eau Rouge . . . pouhons springs: in the Belgian Ardennes, which Apollinaire knew well from having spent the summer of 1899 there with his brother. 'Pouhons' is the local word for the region's mineral springs.

I shall never forget: the calligramme contains an untranslatable play on the words *vers* and *versailles*.

And when after having passed that afternoon: Apollinaire made a short halt in Fontainebleau, where he wrote a prose description of his journey, published in 1921, 'La Fête Manquée'.

'In Nîmes'

Written in December 1914 while Apollinaire was based in Nîmes. Émile Léonard was a fellow soldier. In March Apollinaire requested a transfer to the front and was sent to Champagne.

In Nîmes' Ninth Convoy: the 'Charroi de Nîmes' is the title of a twelfth-century French chanson de geste.

Tour Magne: Magne (Great) Tower is the only remaining tower of Nîmes' Roman walls.

'Night Watch'

In an early version of this poem 'troudla' is abbreviated 'T. du c.' (*trou du cul*: arsehole), and it is used as a refrain. The poem was sent on 13 March 1915 to André Rouveyre, the owner of 'The Little Auto'.

Troudla la Champignon Tabatière: roughly translated as 'Arse-hole Mushroom Snuff Box'.

Mercure de France: a French literary magazine and (now) publishing house whose history begins in the seventeenth century. Apollinaire was a columnist.

graph paper: papier quadrillé. No French schoolchild escapes a paper fetish as, at the start of each school year, their teachers send home long lists of school supplies to be purchased. Cultural artifacts, the lists inevitably specify several different kinds of paper, loose or in notebooks: *grand format, petit format, copies simples, copies doubles, perforés, à spirales, à petits carreaux, à grands carreaux*. Stationeries and supermarkets are taken by storm. Apollinaire, the record shows, was a studious boy, who won many prizes.

'Shadow'

Philippe Soupault writes (1926): 'One day I asked Apollinaire for a poem . . . he disappeared into the back of the apartment and three hours later reappeared and handed me the poem "Ombre".'

Olive of time: cf Shakespeare's Sonnet 107, 'And peace proclaims olives of endless age.'

A god who humbles himself: Un dieu qui s'humilie. S'humilier might also mean 'to humiliate oneself.' *Humble, humiliate,* from Latin *humilis,* 'low, lowly', from *humus,* 'ground'.

'Reconnaissance'

'Reconnaissance' is dedicated to Madeleine Pagès, a young woman whom Apollinaire met on 2 January 1915 on a train to Marseille, then corresponded with on an almost daily basis from the front. In August they became engaged, although the engagement was later broken off. The poem was also sent to Louise de Coligny-Châtillon ('Lou' in several poems of the *Calligrammes*), whom Apollinaire had met in Nice in 1914. In the May 1915 letter to Madeleine, in which this poem was included, Apollinaire describes crawling 'on our bellies' through trenches as German shells exploded around them. A few days earlier he had written her 'sitting on a bag of oats', seeing the sky through trees 'like a blue-black eye immense and faithful'.

'14 June 1915'

On 20 June 1915 Apollinaire wrote Madeleine, "Two weeks without writing, impossible! . . . We changed sector – I'm not in the 59th any more but the 69th.' In the first edition (*Case d'Armons*, a pamphlet published at the front), Apollinaire dedicated this poem to his mother.

La Marseillaise de Rude: François Rude's sculpture, 'Departure of the Volunteers of '92', also known as 'La Marseillaise', decorates the Arc de Triomphe in Paris.

'The Sighs of the Dakar Gunner'

This poem is unique in *Calligrammes* in being spoken by a Senegalese gunner, who contrasts life on the battlefront with life in Senegal, and speaks with great poignancy of colonial intrusions into West African traditions: wars on the Gold Coast, the missionary-priest, sexual slavery, servitude in Europe. The poem also reminds us of the Cubists' and Surrealists' interest in the ethnology and arts of Africa.

Doughboys: in French 'bobosses' which, Apollinaire wrote to Madeleine Pagès, was a tenderly comic diminutive of 'fantabosses,' or 'fantassins à bosses': gunners, humpbacked by their packs.

'April Night 1915'

This poem, with its mixture of melancholy and celebration, was the closing poem in the pamphlet *Case d'Armons*. It is dedicated to Louise de Coligny-Châtillon.

Heart burst shell you whistled your romance: Apollinaire wrote 'Lou': 'I don't hate it that Love sometimes makes me suffer. It's a source of poetry that never runs dry.'

It's raining dead eyes: Apollinaire often uses eye images for exploding shells, for instance at the end of 'The Sighs of the Dakar Gunner'.

'Grace Exiled', 'Bivouac Fires', 'Swarm of Flies', 'The Horseman's Farewell'

These poems were part of a sequence of seven poems written by Apollinaire to illustrate drawings by Marie Laurencin.

'The Thunder's Palace'

Sent to Madeleine Pagès on 11 October 1915. On 2 September, in response to one of her letters he'd written, '. . .The old taste needs to be turned upside down. So, yesterday in a dugout I saw a ham, partly carved, it was ravishing, a violin on a wall is marvellous and I thought that one of the prettiest ways of decorating a bedroom would be to wallpaper it with lots of different kinds of newspapers.' On 5 October, however, Apollinaire wrote Madeleine, 'I'm writing badly because I feel bad. It's cold, during the day we can't light a fire because of the smoke so we can't write. In the evening each group of gunners crowds into its hole. We light a fire. But the men are here, playing cards and joking.'

'Photograph'

Sent to Madeleine Pagès, after receiving her photograph, on 13 October 1915. In the same letter he sent another poem he called '4 a.m.':

> It's 4 in the morning
> I get up completely dressed
> I have a cake of soap
> A person I love sent me
> I'm going to wash
> I leave the hole we sleep in
> I feel good
> I'm glad I can wash it's the first time in three days
> Once I've washed I'm going to shave
> After that sky blue I fade into the horizon until night and it's a very
>   sweet pleasure
> To say nothing more, everything I do an invisible being is doing
> Since once buttoned up the same blue as the sky I become invisible

In 1915, with the start of trench warfare, the French army introduced its famous 'horizon-blue' uniform and metal helmets, replacing the obsolete brightly coloured uniform and cloth 'kepi' headgear. On 4 June 1915, Apollinaire wrote to Madeleine, 'The superstition about blue delightfully unites us and when I imagine your heart I colour it blue . . .'

'The English Inscription'

Sent to Madeleine Pagès 28 May 1915 with the title 'Madeleine', the poem's opening lines recall Apollinaire's chance meeting with her in January 1915 on a train between Nice and Marseilles.

Whose every letter curls: 'curls' (weakly) translates Apollinaire's wordplay on the French verb 'love' ('to coil up') and the English meaning of the same four letters.

in a beautiful round English hand: English penmanship was thought in France to be particularly full and rounded.

'In the Cave-Shelter'

Sent to Madeleine Pagès 8 October 1915.

stearin: wax, or tallow for candles, from rendered animal fat (from slaughterhouses).

'Flare'

Sent to Madeleine Pagès 9 October 1915. On the 8th Apollinaire had written an impassioned letter describing Madeleine's forehead, earlobe and 'the wonderful thickness of your long black hair', followed by a quotation from a poem by Baudelaire. He also wrote about his jealousy, 'about all the people around you . . .even the big pupils in your class who must be a little in love with their adorable teacher.' (Madeleine was a secondary-school teacher of French language and literature in Oran, Algeria.)

Flare: flares were rockets sent up to burn brightly so as to light up men and other targets in the area between the front lines.

'Desire'

Sent to Madeleine Pagès 6 October 1915. In his letter Apollinaire wrote,

'I'm sending you lines that I wrote after writing you yesterday evening and you'll have an idea of my splenetic state. Today much work, attack, they say, tomorrow, after which I really hope we'll occupy a position beyond the Boche lines. [. . .]' He asked Madeleine to make fair copies of his poems that he could submit to magazines.

Butte du Mesnil: beginning in September 1915, intense fighting took place around the village of Mesnil-les-Hurlus in Champagne-Ardennes. The Butte de Mesnil with its system of trenches was only retaken by the French forces in September 1918. The village, which had 97 inhabitants in 1911, was destroyed. The ruins of its thirteenth-century church were excavated in 1984.

Decauville: Decauville was a French company that built light railways. These had civil and military uses, including the transportation of artillery pieces and ammunition. Decauville built thousands of miles of trench railways track for the French and the British during World War I.

my bourguignotte: Originally from Burgundy, the *bourguignotte* was a helmet used in the fifteenth and sixteenth centuries. In World War I it gave its name to the combat helmet *(casque Adrian)* issued to the infantry, because of the injuries they were sustaining in trench warfare from exploding shells. The Adrian helmet was the first modern steel helmet.

Main de Massiges: this was the location of a major fight in Champagne in 1915. *Main* means 'hand'.

Goethe Trench . . . Nietzsche's trench: soldiers named their own trenches and those of the enemy. Some sections of British trenches, for instance, were called 'Bond Street', or 'Black Watch Alley'; and British soldiers gave German trenches names like 'Beer Trench' or 'Ale Alley'.

Night of September 24: 25 September was the date of this major battle.

'Ocean of Earth'

Apollinaire, perhaps because of his Mediterranean youth, was fascinated by octopuses, which he also mentions in 'Zone'; lemon trees are also a frequent image.

Giorgio de Chirico had been noticed by Apollinaire when De Chirico moved to Paris; Apollinaire, who wrote art criticism, helped him find a gallery. De Chirico painted *Premonitory Portrait of Apollinaire* (1914, Centre Pompidou, Paris); he also illustrated a limited edition of *Calligrammes* (1930). It is thought that De Chirico and Apollinaire influenced one another, in their imagery of women, of tall buildings and smokestacks. De Chirico enlisted in the Italian army in 1915, but was found unfit for active duty and assigned to the Ferrara hospital.

Watch out we're going to drop our inkers / Watch out for the ink we splot: in French Apollinaire puns on the similar sound of *encre* (ink) and *ancre* (anchor).

'Wonder of War'

Dated December 1915. Flares (*fusées*) were used to light up battlegrounds by night: '. . . hard spurts of light shot across the sky actors incredibly thinned out that came close faded loomed up shrunk flares signals raining down in sprays globes persisting white orange red blue green rose singular exquisite dancers,' Apollinaire wrote to Madeleine Pagès on 2 September 1915.

all my Berenices: Berenice, 'the Queen of Palestine', is a character in a play of the same name by the seventeenth-century French playwright Racine and a symbol of the passionately loved woman.

ponytails: in French, 'chevelures', a word to describe hair, with a suggestion of length and abundance, and one difficult to translate into modern English. 'Locks'? 'Mane'? I've used the anachronistic 'ponytails' as fitting the immediately following image of comets.

a giorno: in Italian in the original, meaning 'bright as day'.

trenches: *boyaux* in French; the primary meaning of *boyaux* is 'guts,' 'entrails', from Latin *botellus*, 'little sausage'.

I leave to the future the story of Guillaume Apollinaire / Who went to war and knew how to be everywhere: these and the following lines recall Apollinaire's Cubist aesthetic of Simultaneity, or the ability of one's thoughts to be many places/times at once.

'Basic Training'

Sent to Madeleine Pagès on 22 November 1915, two days before Apollinaire's promotion to the rank of infantry officer. Called *Exercice* in French, the poem is rhymed abab cdcd efef and has a witty, poignant and untranslatable wordplay on the words *ascèse* (ascesis) and *exercice* (in the sense of military training but also, ironically, training for death).

'There's'

Sent to Madeleine 30 September 1915.

tripe: in French *boyaux*, 'intestines', but also 'the trenches', these particular ones named after German writers and cities.

letter: in the first draft of the poem, this line said 'a letter from Madeleine'.

TSF: *télégraphie sans fil*: the wireless.

Mexico . . . Algeria: Apollinaire's brother was living in Mexico; Madeleine lived in Algeria. (Note, again, the juxtaposition of many different experiences.)

'The Grape Grower in Champagne'

Sent to Madeleine on 7 February 1916, this poem was written in Hautvilliers, in the heart of Champagne, where Apollinaire's regiment had been sent for a rest. In the letter that accompanied the poem Apollinaire wrote, 'This being the birthplace of Champagne 2 centuries ago, the wine is good and we drink it . . . I think it's going to rain, if we return early I'll try my hand at a poem. It's unbelievable how little time one has for oneself in the infantry. Think how many poems finished in the artillery and how many in the infantry maybe not one . . .'

'Postcard'

Sent on a postcard to André Rouveyre (owner of 'the little auto') on 20 August 1915.

The second and last lines of this poem, which rhymes abcabc, end with the word *été*, meaning in the first instance 'summer' and in the second 'been', past participle of the verb to be.

'The Future'

Sent to Madeleine on 11 March 1916. Apollinaire's regiment, still resting, was to move back to the front on 14 March. On the 10th he wrote, 'I saw the royal city [Reims], its cathedral and I picked up some shards of stained glass . . . the rose window which was so beautiful has been partly destroyed by the fire . . . We leave tomorrow for the front.' (By March 1916 Apollinaire's correspondence with Madeleine, though still affectionate, had become less frequent and less impassioned.)

gabions: wicker containers, without a bottom, filled with earth or stone and used in fortifications.

'Chevaux-de-frise'

Sent to Madeleine on 18 November 1915: 'Yesterday evening we headed off in the snow, shell holes, then the Boche trenches the countryside changing suddenly, finally some big bony and often broken trees. [. . .] Around our shelters, a large Germany cemetery, almost all the tombs date from February . . . I'm fine in my bed off in the corner, I make myself a little alcove, cut off by a sheet of canvas.'

cheval-de-frise: a portable military obstacle made of wood and barbed wire. So Apollinaire is playing on correspondences between bare, broken trees, barricades, and real horses, as on 'barbed' and 'Barb'.

Barb horses: the Barb horse, developed on the Barbary coast of North Africa in the eighth century, is a light, tough riding horse.

the Paraclete: the Holy Spirit.

your beautiful Orient: Madeleine lived in Algeria.

'Platoon Leader'

Dated March 1916, this poem had been sent to Madeleine in an earlier version, 'Le Quatrième Poème Secret' ('The Fourth Secret Poem'), on 19 October 1915. In the earlier version Apollinaire analyses a photograph of Madeleine that he has just received.

'Victory'

Apollinaire was wounded on 17 March 1916 and evacuated to Paris. This poem was first published on 15 March 1917. 'Home' probably refers to Apollinaire's apartment at 202 boulevard Saint-Germain.

punctured helmet: Apollinaire's head wound was the result of shrapnel piercing his helmet.

Saint-Claude: a town in the Jura Mountains of France known for its gem-cutting and briar pipes.

Eros and Anteros: winged gods of love. Anteros was the god of requited, or counter, love.

Hydra of Lerna: ancient snake-like beast with many heads, killed by Hercules as the second of his twelve labours.

'The Pretty Redhead'

This poem, inspired by Jacqueline Kolb, whom Apollinaire was about to marry (on 2 May 1918), was published in March 1918 in a Swiss review, *L'Éventail*. It is the last poem in his collection *Calligrammes,* published in April 1918, and his poetic testament.

In November 1918 Apollinaire died in Paris, having come down with flu during the pandemic.

Ⓑ *editions*

Founded in 2007, CB editions publishes chiefly short
fiction (including work by Gabriel Josipovici, Todd
McEwen and David Markson) and poetry (Fergus
Allen, Andrew Elliott, Beverley Bie Brahic, Nancy
Gaffield, J. O. Morgan, D. Nurkse). Writers published
in translation include Apollinaire, Andrzej Bursa,
Joaquín Giannuzzi, Gert Hofmann and Francis Ponge.

Books can be ordered from www.cbeditions.com.